Dr. Mark H. Ballard

WITH DR. TIMOTHY CHRISTIAN

Priorities

Reaching the Life
God Intended

ISBN 978-1-0980-0585-6 (paperback)
ISBN 978-1-0980-0586-3 (digital)

Christian Faith Publishing, Inc.
832 Park Avenue
Meadville, PA 16335
www.christianfaithpublishing.com

Printed in the United States of America

Contents

Introduction

"I don't want to sound like a nag," I said.

"Then don't." He didn't smile.

It wasn't his characteristic, *deflect with humor* comment.

"If no one else cares enough to tell you," I continued, "I do." I paused, trying not to sound harsh or judgmental. "Here it is. You've got to get your priorities straight. It's that simple."

Defiance flashed in his eyes. He resisted. Then he softened, exhaled, and leaned forward, palms down on the bathroom vanity.

"You're right," he said. "I don't like it, but I know it's true."

I washed the shave cream residue from his face and combed his hair. "Today's the day," I said. "Get to it."

Sounds familiar? Ever had a similar *come to Jesus moment* in your bathroom mirror?

Whether you've had the uncomfortable moment with yourself or someone else, priorities are crucial. No one has unlimited time, talents, or treasures.

Time

We all have the same amount of time. No one gets more than twenty-four hours in a day or seven days in a week.

On top of that, life is fragile. Tomorrow is uncertain. We either use our time or lose our time. Priorities help us invest precious time wisely.

Talents

We all have talents. Some have many, others have few. No one can do everything. We must make choices.

How will you use your God-given talents? Priorities will help you invest those talents in what is most important.

Treasures

Likewise, we all have treasures. Some are wealthy. Some have just enough. Some struggle, always seeming to run out of money before running out of month. Yet even the wealthiest have limited resources. All of us must make choices.

How will you spend your treasures? Priorities will help you invest in what is most important.

Is it easy for you to set priorities or is it difficult? Even those who find it easy face bigger challenges,

- living their priorities,
- evaluating their priorities regularly, and
- sticking with them for the long-term.

Personal Experience

I was fortunate. My introduction to priorities began early.

I attended Parkhill Christian Academy from the middle of my second-grade year through high school graduation. The school's educational system engrained priority setting into my life.

Unfortunately, I was a slow learner. My first several years at Parkhill were difficult. I drifted through elementary and middle school, indifferent to the school's *priority* training. I set the lowest possible priorities then ignored them.

The results were as predictable as the lunar cycle. My grades were poor. I lagged behind my classmates. A common assessment of my potential was "I don't think he'll ever graduate from high school." However, my parents, my teachers, and a principal refused to give up on me.

In the ninth grade, things changed. All the effort and energy those caring adults invested in me finally paid off. The idea of priorities sank in. I learned to set meaningful, measurable, achievable goals. I learned to develop action steps to reach those goals. I also learned to evaluate my progress and make the necessary adjustments to achieve my goals.

Before I realized it, for the first time in my life, I caught up to and excelled from the rest of my classmates. In a single year, I completed the ninth and half of the tenth grade.

The next year, I made equal progress.

Living by priorities began to transform my life. It was a great benefit at the time. Living out my priorities has proven even more helpful through more than thirty years of ministry.

During my first year of high school, my dad was forced to take an early retirement due to downsizing of the company he served for more than thirty-three years. He began experiencing health problems. Then shortly after my second year of high school, my mother died. My dad was devastated. Debilitating depression overwhelmed him. If we were going to make it financially, I had to contribute to the household income.

Because of my academic achievements during the first two years of high school, I was able to cut my school hours to a half day and increase my work hours. I stretched my final year over two years and graduated with my class. This would not have been possible if I had not learned to prioritize my life.

The lessons I learned about priorities, goals, action plans, evaluation, and adjustment have served me well throughout life. In fact, I still use the principles I learned back in 1982. Over the years, the Lord has allowed me to help others learn about setting priorities. Several have asked me to put the most important lessons into a book. That repeated request inspired the following pages.

While I have not included everything I have learned about priorities in this little book, I have included what I believe to be the most important. The lessons came from two sources primarily: First, they came from God's Word. The Bible teaches us more about priorities than any other book. Second, the material represents my personal experience living out the biblical principles. Of course, as stated above, my foundation for discovering biblical priorities was laid back at Park Hill Christian Academy.

I pray that as you read these pages, the Father will help you evaluate your priorities. I also trust He will help you adjust your life to live out His priorities for you. Once the adjustments are made, the real work has just begun!

We all are tempted to ignore our priorities. So we will also consider how to continue living our priorities even when it is difficult. Further, we will note the blessing of faithfully living God's priorities for our lives.

One suggestion as we begin: prioritize reading and applying one chapter a week for the next five weeks, ask God to show you what He wants you to learn, then read a chapter. Think about the chapter. Pray about the chapter. Reflect on the chapter. Ask the Lord what He wants you to do about it. Respond in a way that pleases Him. In order to help you reflect and respond, an application section will conclude each chapter.

Let's get started.

Chapter 1

Examining Your Priorities

I am not only the founding president but also a professor at Northeastern Baptist College in Bennington, Vermont. It isn't my favorite part of the job, but giving examinations is one of my responsibilities. Also, I have made it my personal responsibility to take exams regularly.

Students tend to forget much of the examination material as soon as an exam is over. We call that "downloading" or "dumping." The material studied goes directly from the brain to the test paper, and there it remains to be remembered no more.

I will admit to some personal experience with *downloading* a time or two in my four years of college and seven years of graduate school. However, I take a particular examination on a regular basis, and I never want to forget the questions or my answers. This exam has been very helpful in numerous ways.

Today I invite you to take the same exam. You do not need to study ahead of time.

Also, your answers may differ from anyone else's. They should be personal and individual. We are not trying to make a passing grade but please God. We are discovering where we've come from, where we are, and where we're going in life. Today I invite you to examine your priorities.

Exam Instructions: Fold a blank piece of paper in half. On the left side, write the top five to ten priorities you desire for your life. Carefully examine your list. These should be your aspirational priorities. They state the way you aspire to live. When you are certain your list reflects the priorities you truly desire, set it aside and read this chapter. Later we will return to the list.

Right life priorities lead to successful living. Unfortunately, we all struggle with priorities.

Many never stop to list their priorities. They have priorities (everyone does, realize it or not), but their life is unexamined. It is as if they are walking through the dark room of a fun house. They bump into other people and things. They hit brick walls, bounce off, and continue groping in the dark.

Others list their priorities but rarely examine them. They never ask if they are actually living those priorities.

For example, most Christians believe our churches need revival. We believe the nation needs an awakening. Yet few consider their life priorities in light of that belief.

The problem is not new. God's people have always struggled with life priorities. We believe right. We want to do right. Yet somehow, we fail to align our lives with God's priorities.

What happens when God's people have misplaced priorities? What does God do about our misplaced priorities? In other words, how do you know if you have gotten off track and drifted away?

A vivid example is found in the events surrounding Haggai's prophecies. God gave His people a clear priority assignment. They understood. They were neither in the dark nor in doubt. Yet their priorities were misplaced.

God dealt with the problem in three ways. I believe we'll see a similar pattern in our lives today.

Confrontation

Some historical perspective will help us.

Eighty-six years before Haggai came on the scene, the southern kingdom of Judah went into captivity. From the time Israel divided into two kingdoms, the southern kingdom followed a pattern. They would turn to the Lord for a period of time, usually during a godly king's reign in conjunction with a Spirit anointed priest or prophet's ministry. God's Word was proclaimed faith-fully, and God's people obeyed.

During those times, God blessed the nation. They were prosperous and protected.

Inevitably the leaders died, and spiritual drift set in. Personal priorities began to replace God's priorities. The people turned away from the Lord. Though the Southern Kingdom maintained outward religious rituals throughout their history, the Lord Himself charged, "Your heart is far from me."

Syncretism

A syncretized religion was introduced. It suggested one could have the best of both worlds; one could serve God and idols; one could maintain temple rituals, receive God's blessings, and enjoy the pleasures and benefits of idol worship on the side.

Rebellion, Revival Cycle

God's prophets exposed syncretism for the lie it was. Under a prophet's ministry in conjunction with a godly wise king, God's people awakened. They turned to the Lord and away from idolatry. Revival continued as long as the godly leaders lived. A period of spiritual drift followed, resulting in spiritual rebellion. God's chastening followed then a new prophet, and the cycle continued. Revival. Rebellion. Revival. Rebellion.

As the years passed and the cycle continued, the revivals weakened. The nation's repentance was not as complete as before and their faithfulness not as enduring. Rebellion became deeper as well.

The syncretistic religion, once disdained, began to be tolerated. Then it became acceptable. Then it became popular. Then predominate. What was once feared was celebrated, and what was once celebrated was condemned. Good became evil and evil became good. Sound familiar?

God Responds

God continued to send multiple warnings through His prophets. Eventually, the nation refused to repent, and God faithfully fulfilled His warnings.

God will not compromise the first of His ten commandments: "You shall have no other gods before Me" (Exod. 20:3). Israel's children refused to prioritize their relationship with Yahweh. Therefore, God delivered them into the hands of Nebuchadnezzar and the Babylonian Empire. The nation went into Babylonian captivity in 606 BC. As promised, their captivity continued for seventy years.

God Remembers

Still, God never forgot His promises to Abraham, Isaac, Israel, and David. The Lord promised to raise up a new leader after the seventy years. Not an Israeli leader but a foreign monarch. The leader's name would be Cyrus, and he would send the Jews back to Jerusalem. Cyrus would also command them to rebuild God's Temple (Isa. 44:28).

So it happened. As the seventieth year of Jewish captivity approached, the Persians invaded and conquered Babylon. Cyrus came to power as prophesied. Sixteen years before Haggai published his book (536 BC), Cyrus issued a decree for the Jews to return to Jerusalem and rebuild the temple.

Be encouraged. God's Word will always be fulfilled.

Jews Returned

The Jews returned to their homeland with great excitement and anticipation. Most had not seen Solomon's Temple; they were born in captivity. A few, however, had seen it. They remembered the temple's former glory. No doubt they told the younger people about it.

For those who settled in Jerusalem, the devastation was overwhelming. The walled city was in ruins. The temple they were to rebuild was nothing but rubble. There was no gold, silver, or wood. A few scattered foundation stones remained, but they were covered with debris.

The people arrived in country with a God-given priority and action plans to complete their assignment.

They began to work, but opposition soon arose. Enemies petitioned the Persian king to stop their work. They claimed the Jews were organizing a rebellion. To make matters worse, the available resources were being used up quickly. It was certain the Persian king would not send more aid. Since the task was hard, the resources were few, the opposition was intense, and no help was on the horizon, the work ceased.

No doubt the delay concerned the Jews at first. The elderly must have warned them that misplaced priorities led to the nation's original demise and the temple's destruction. They never completely abandoned the idea of rebuilding the temple. They just procrastinated.

Delay Justified

For a while, the topic came up often. "We must rebuild the temple. God promised He would send us back to do it, and He did. We're here. Let's do it."

Everyone agreed. "You're right. It has to be done. It can be done. But..."

Rebuilding was perpetually postponed; it was not a priority.

A common saying ended every reconstruction conversation: "The time has not come, the time that the LORD's house should be built."

God understands. You and I face many challenges. Many things distract, discourage, and derail us from fulfilling His purpose for our lives, our families, and our churches. He knows we are facing opposition, limited resources, and hard work. Even so, He expects us to make His priorities our priorities. When our priorities are misplaced, He confronts us. And so it happened in Jerusalem.

Misplaced Priorities

Sixteen years passed. The returned Jews had not managed to remove the rubble or complete the temple's foundation. Rebuilding was rarely mentioned anymore. When it was, some said, "I agree. We'll do it…when the time's right. But not yet. When God removes the obstacles, we'll begin."

Haggai's First Sermon

Haggai arrived on the scene. He confronted the people with God's message. "This people say, 'The time has not come, the time that the Lord's house be built.' Then the word of the Lord came by Haggai the prophet saying, 'Is it time for you yourselves to dwell in your paneled houses, and this Temple to lie in ruins?'" (1:2–4).

The Lord did not sugarcoat His message neither did the prophet. Haggai delivered what He received.

The Jews never removed rebuilding the temple from their priority list. But it was an aspirational priority, not an actual priority. They never scheduled or implemented their action plans.

During those years, however, they were not idle. Despite the hard work, opposition, and lack of resources, the people found ways to plant crops, develop businesses, and build their own houses. In fact, they built *paneled houses*. The Hebrew word is *caphan*. The old King James Version translated it, *ceiled*. The word means "to be covered over with a nice finish." We might think of covering the walls with an expensive wainscoting or carefully milled wood panels.

Misplaced Priorities Succeed

Nice houses were not the problem. The problem was that while they built nice houses for themselves, the temple lay *in ruins*. Misplaced priorities can succeed. They are achievable.

Jerusalem's returned residents had a priority problem, not an obstacle problem. Yes, there were challenges to rebuilding the temple. But despite the challenges, they accomplished their actual priorities—building their own houses. The Lord's work was moved down the priority list. "The time has not come to build the Lord's house."

God did not allow His people to continue in their misplaced priorities. He confronted them.

I'm personally familiar with the problem and the confrontation.

My Uncomfortable Confrontation

It was a beautiful September morning in the fall of 2009. After a great morning devotional time with the Lord, I headed to the church to begin a busy week. My worship time spilled over into the thirty-minute drive to the church. I sang praises to the Lord as I drove down I-93. Getting off at exit 5 in North Londonderry, I was not ready for the time with the Lord to end. I pulled off the highway and spent more time praying and singing praises to the Lord.

After a little while, as I merged back into traffic, I said, "Father, thank you so much for all You have done and are doing! Thank you for my wife, my son, the church, and all that you are accomplishing in this town."

Immediately, an old but familiar thought popped into my mind, *Mark, you are too comfortable.* The Lord had used the same thought to prepare me to move to New England almost twelve years earlier.

I did not like the thought. I said, "Lord, it's about time I enjoyed a little comfort. Cindy and I have put in our time of sacrifice. Father, we came here with nothing and we still have nothing. But finally, we're receiving consistent paychecks. Lord, we have a son now. We have new responsibilities. We can't even contemplate another *uncomfortable* move. Lord, I like being just a little comfortable." Then I pushed the thought from my mind.

In that one moment, I went from praise and submission, to adjusting my priority list. I did not remove *obeying God* from my priority list. I just shifted it down a bit. My comfort and my family's comfort moved ahead on my priority list. In that moment, my priorities were misplaced.

The Father always *confronts* misplaced priorities. It wasn't constant. It wasn't even daily. But several times throughout the month, the Lord gently brought me back to that moment. He reminded me of my misplaced priorities. Each time, I offered a few excuses and put it out of my mind. But God's confrontation intensified.

Throughout October, the internal struggle grew. The Father reminded me of many things He had done over the years to prepare me for that specific moment in time. Each time the confrontation grew, the Lord's conviction became more difficult to ignore. The issue came to a head during the final weekend of October.

The Lord made it abundantly clear that He was calling me to leave the comfort of a secure pastorate and step out in faith to start Northeastern Baptist College. While the battle within had gone on for well over a month by this point, I had not told my wife, Cindy, about my struggle. Why? Every time God called us to step out in faith to less or no salary in the past, Cindy was supportive. When I shared such a struggle, Cindy said, "Well, I don't know how we'll make it, but if God is calling us, we must do it. He will provide somehow." Those words encouraged me in the past. This time, the thought of hearing Cindy say it scared me. So I kept the struggle to myself.

On Friday night of the final weekend in October, we held a one-night revival service at our church. A friend came to preach the service. The next day, he was to lead a pastoral counseling training seminar for some of the pastors in our association. He would again preach at our church on Sunday.

My friend, Marvin Jones, preached a great message on Friday night. Repeatedly, throughout the sermon, I said, "Amen!" The Holy Spirit spoke to me. "What about you? Why won't you surrender to my call?" The confrontation intensified.

As I arrived to set up for the Saturday seminar, I thought, *At least, I'm safe today. Marvin is teaching these guys about counseling.*

At some point during every session, however, Marvin stopped his instruction. He said something like, "This has nothing to do with the topic at hand, but men, I believe the Lord wants me to say something to you." He chased an apparent rabbit trail but he was hot on my trail. He spoke directly to me, though he didn't know it. I couldn't wait for the day to end.

Saturday night, I told Cindy, "I think the Lord is calling us to step out in faith and start a Baptist college to train students to impact the Northeast with the gospel. Cindy, we have no money. This will be the most difficult thing we have ever done. If we attempt this, I have no idea how we will survive, much less open a college."

Cindy replied, "Mark, I don't know how we can make it either, but if God is calling us, we must do it. He will provide somehow. Just be sure God is calling. If He is, let's do it." The very response I feared!

During Marvin's sermon on Sunday morning, I did not utter an "Amen." In fact, I don't know what my friend preached. Through the entire service, God confronted me. I could think of nothing else until I surrendered. Finally I bowed my head and said, "Yes, Lord. I surrender to Your will. Please forgive me for prioritizing my comfort over Your will. With Your help, we will start a Baptist college in New England." And so, we did.

Is the Lord confronting you with misplaced priorities today? If so, the confrontation will not go away. Stop reading now and surrender your priority list to God.

The path may be difficult. Opposition may rise. The resources may be few or even nonexistent. But following God's priorities for your life is always the best path.

When God confronts His people with misplaced priorities, a decision must be made. We either adjust our priorities to match His priorities or we continue to do our own thing. It is crucial to understand that when we refuse to realign our priorities, God does not surrender to our wills. He does not change His mind. Rather He moves from confrontation to correction.

Correction

When God confronts us, as we continue in our misplaced priorities, He corrects us. Hudson Taylor, the great missionary to China and founder of the China Inland Mission, once said, "Every work of God has three stages: first it is difficult, then it is impossible, and then it is done."

Taylor followed the Lord's priorities for his life despite extreme challenges. He constantly lacked resources, but he turned to the Father in prayer. He asked Him to meet his financial needs, and He did. The wisdom expressed in a simple sentence, "First it is difficult, then it is impossible, and then it is done," speaks volumes.

Human wisdom says, "It is difficult, so I won't start," or "It was difficult and now it's impossible. I quit." Such was the case with the Jews who returned to Jerusalem to rebuild the temple. When the difficult work faced serious opposition and a lack of resources, they quit working on the temple. God confronted them, but they still said, "The time has not come, the time that the LORD's house should be built." Therefore, God moved beyond confrontation to correction. Haggai described the Father's corrective measures.

> You have sown much, and bring in little; You eat, but do not have enough; You drink, but you are not filled with drink; You clothe yourselves, but no one is warm; And he who earns wages, earns wages to put into a bag with holes. "You looked

for much, but indeed it came to little; and when you brought it home,
I blew it away. Why?" says the Lord
of hosts. "Because of My house that
is in ruins while every one of you
runs to his own house. Therefore the
heavens above you withhold the dew,
the earth withholds its fruit. For I
called for a drought on the land and
the mountains, on the grain and the
new wine and the oil, on whatever
the ground brings forth, on men and
livestock, and on all the labor of *your*
hands." (Hag. 1:6, 9–11)

Not every trial is rooted in misplaced priorities,
but some are. Some trials are caused by disobedience.
Others, like the trials the Jews encountered when they
first returned to Jerusalem, come from the enemy.

Though we live in the age of grace, we are not
exempted from the enemy's attacks. Satan and his
demons launch spiritual attacks, intended to keep us
from accomplishing the work to which God called us. If
we surrender to trials and jettison God's priorities, things
only get worse.

So it was with the returned exiles in Jerusalem.
They reacted in fear. The difficult work, opposition,
and lack of resources defeated them. They should have
pressed forward in faith. Instead, they took the resources

they had and tried to make themselves as comfortable as possible.

"We will build the temple," they said, "but not now. When God gives us all the silver and gold we need, we'll act. Until then, it's clear the time has not come." As a result, all their attempts at self-protection and comfort failed.

They sowed seed but little grew. They focused on cozy, warmth, comfort, but the cold seeped into their bones. They earned money and secured it in a money pouch. When it was time to pay for a transaction, they discovered a hole and an empty pouch. Opposition was nothing compared to God's correction.

Every time God's people prioritize personal comforts over His commands, things get worse not better. We think we are protecting our families, our church budgets, and personal security. In reality, we are acting in fear and inviting God's correction. He wants us to keep His priorities as our priorities. He wants us to

- obey;
- walk in faith, not fear; and
- trust Him to provide what we lack.

When we choose fear instead of faith, He corrects. So I've learned.

Accommodating Fear

In the summer and fall of 1994, I adjusted my priorities to accommodate my fear. It did not go well. Still, God was gracious. He corrected me and taught me a valuable life lesson.

While in seminary, I pastored a small country church in North Carolina. Cindy and I loved the people, and they loved us. Despite the congregation's petite size, God worked. Several came to faith in Jesus. We enjoyed the ministry. We would have been contented to spend a lifetime, reaching that community.

One Tuesday, a seminary friend urged me to go with him to talk with the visiting representatives from the Home Mission Board of the Southern Baptist Convention. They were on campus recruiting students to spend the following summer starting churches. The program offered church planting field experience and eight hours credit toward the Master of Divinity degree.

"We both planted churches before coming to seminary," my friend said. "We should go talk to them."

I was not interested, but my friend was relentless. He continued to bring it up throughout the day. Finally I said, "Look, I'm happy at my church. I have no intention of leaving it."

My friend seemed to accept my answer but asked me to go with him. He was interested. I agreed.

During the initial conversation, the representative asked if I was interested. My response to her was the same as to my friend. Eventually the conversation turned back to me. My friend explained my previous church planting experience. Before leaving the building, the Home Mission Board representative convinced me to at least pray about the possibility.

At home that night, I shared the experience with Cindy. She said, "Well, Mark, we should at least pray about it. If the Lord leads us to do this, we should. We will just have to trust Him to provide. He's never let us down before." We prayed that night and again the next morning.

Back on campus the next day, I spoke with the representative again. This led to several conversations with leaders from various states and associations. Eventually the Lord confirmed that we were to participate in the summer program. We were assigned to a town in Florida that had no Baptist church.

Next, we faced the difficult task of telling our church. I believed the Lord called us to resign, spend the summer planting a church in Florida, then return to seminary in the fall for my final year of the Master of Divinity program.

Friends asked, "What will you do at the end of the summer?"

We had no idea. I was certain, however, that the Lord had led us to resign and step out in faith, trusting His plan for us in Florida and beyond. Advice flowed in from all directions. Our church did not understand. Our friends did not understand. Even family members questioned our decision. The consistent advice was "Take a leave of absence from your church in North Carolina. Come back at the end of the summer and pick up where you left off."

On our final Sunday with the church, the chairman of the deacons told me they needed to have a business meeting at the conclusion of the service. I expected they planned to form a pastor search committee.

"We are called to order," he began. "One of the deacons has a motion to bring before the church."

Another deacon said, "Mr. Chairman, I make a motion that we refuse our pastor's resignation and give him a leave of absence for the summer. He can go start a church in Florida and return in the fall to serve as our pastor."

The motion was seconded. They voted by standing affirmation. It was unanimous.

I sat there in shock. I did not know what to say. I was overwhelmed with their love and support. All the advice I had received came flooding into my mind. From a human perspective, there was only one possible response. I had to say *yes*. But deep inside, I was convinced this was not God's leading. I did not know what to do.

Finally, I spoke. "Thank you. You are so gracious, and we love you. I cannot give you an answer. Cindy and I need to pray about this. I do not know what the Lord has for us in the fall. He only showed us that we were to resign and go to Florida for the summer. We will pray and I will contact the chairman of deacons with our answer by Wednesday night."

The pressure continued to build.

On Wednesday, I called the chairman, "I still don't know what the Lord has for us in the fall. All the advice I have received tells me we should accept the church's gracious offer. We have decided to accept with one condition. We do not know what the Lord has in store. We may stay here only a few weeks or months or it may be for the long term. We simply do not know. I want to be sure the church understands that."

"That works for us," he said. "Go with our blessing. Come back and be our pastor." While the decision eased the pressure of the moment, deep down I knew that we exchanged the Lord's leading for comfort. We exchanged His priority for the preference of others and we did it out of fear.

The summer went well. In ten weeks, we visited every home in the small town, started a children's ministry, a weekly Bible study, and prepared for the launch service of the new church. God blessed the work tremendously.

A couple weeks before our time in Florida ended, we received a phone call from a church in Virginia. They had received my résumé. The interesting thing was I had not put out a résumé since before becoming pastor of the church in North Carolina. The résumé had a phone number from several years earlier. When they could not reach us, they moved on to other résumés. But my name kept coming back to the search committee. They tried to find us again. Once again, they could not track us down and they moved on. The Lord continued to bring my name back to the prayerful committee. Eventually, they found our number in Florida.

Two days later, we had a conference call interview. It went well. We hung up the phone, and I looked at Cindy. "Cindy, that is where God wants us to be, and I have blown it by agreeing to return to North Carolina."

Sure enough, the chairman of the committee called later and wanted to know if I would consider coming to Virginia for a second interview and to preach in view of call. I shared our situation and said, "I really do not know what God is going to do with this, but I need to be true to my word and return to North Carolina."

"Why don't you all pray about it, and if the Lord leads, call me in a month or two." He agreed.

The return to our church in North Carolina was a joyful reunion. The Lord provided a furnished house for us to rent.

Before long, we were busy with my last year of seminary and serving the church. However, we were miserable. The Father's correcting hand was upon us. He met our basic needs, but life was hard. We loved our church family, but we knew we were not supposed to be there.

At night, I sat on the front porch, looking out over a field as the sun set and the stars and fireflies appeared. I prayed, "Lord, I blew it. You have put me on a shelf. You will never use me to lead this church forward, and I have missed out on the church You had for me to lead. Father, please be merciful to me."

I was certain we would never hear from Virginia again. However, our God is gracious, full of mercy and compassion.

One night, our landlord came down the dusty road to our house. "You have a phone call up at the big house," he said.

We could not afford a phone. We had given our landlord's number to several people in case we were needed. I went up to his house and answered the extension in his garage.

The chairman of the pastor search committee from Virginia said, "We have prayed, and we believe you are God's man for our church. Would you please come speak to the committee in person and preach in view of a call?"

The Father graciously gave us the opportunity to adjust our priorities. We surrendered to His leading once again.

Before long, we were living and serving in Virginia. Amazingly, this church became what I call "my Philippi." Though we have served in many capacities over the years, this church remains special to this day.

As the Church of Philippi was Paul's partner in the Gospel for life, so Deerfield Baptist Church became our partner for life. Even today, a member of Deerfield serves on the board of trustees of Northeastern Baptist College. Several members have been on mission trips to serve with us.

God has a plan that will last for a lifetime. I almost missed it because I acted out of fear, trying to watch out for my own comfort. Our gracious Father forgave me and put me back on the path of following His priorities for my life.

If today you find yourself under God's correcting hand, turn back to Him. If you have exchanged His priorities for your own comfort, repent. Acknowledge your sin. He will forgive. He will use you again. Adjust your priorities and watch how He will move.

Commands

When our priorities are misplaced, the Lord confronts us, corrects us, and commands us to adjust our priorities. Notice how this happened in ancient Jerusalem.

In the middle of his first sermon, Haggai declared, "Thus says the LORD of hosts, 'Consider your ways! Go up to the mountains and bring wood and build the Temple that I may take pleasure in it and be glorified,' says the LORD" (1:7–8).

The Lord commanded His people to adjust their priorities and get back on track to fulfilling His call on their lives. Notice that the three-part command included action plans.

Available Resources

First, gather the available resources. This is interesting. A lack of resources was one reason the people stopped working on the temple sixteen years earlier. Now as a consequence, the Lord was taking away their limited resources and comforts little by little. Even so, God called attention to the available resources.

I imagine some of those who had seen Solomon's Temple thought, "What? Gather wood? Seriously? Doesn't Haggai know that wood isn't enough to do this job? Has no one told him the wood must be overlaid with silver and gold? We have no silver! We have no gold!"

Too often, we focus on what we do not have when God wants us to use what we do have.

If you go to Israel today and stand on the Temple Mount, you cannot help but see the irony in this text. God's people neglected working on the temple for nearly sixteen years.

"We can't rebuild," they said. "We want to. And we will. When the time's right…but not now. We don't have the necessary supplies."

Then Haggai arrived. "Turn around," he said. "Look, just over there across the Kidron Valley. The Mount of Olives is covered with wood. Stop worrying about what you don't have! Go over there and gather the wood God has already provided."

God did not mention the silver and gold. They did not need it at that point. One needs no wall covering when one has no walls.

Are you struggling with a lack of resources? I understand. Believe me. But are you using what the Lord has already provided? Just as He commanded the Jews, so the Lord calls us to gather the available resources and put them to work in His service now.

Work

The second part of the command is simple: "Get to work! Stop talking about what you intend to do someday. Organize the woodchoppers and wood haulers and go to work." Next after transporting the wood to the site, "build the temple."

Too often, God's children talk about the need for work. We train ourselves in different ways to get to work. We pray about working. We even say, "The need is urgent. We must get to work." But we do not do any work.

God's command is clear. No more delay! Get to work!

Glorify God

The result of obeying God's command leads to the third part of His command: "Glorify Me!" When God's people stop delaying, gather the resources, and get to work, God is glorified. He said it. "Build the temple, and I will 'take pleasure in it and be glorified.'"

Do you want to glorify God? Of course, you do. Every Christian does. The good news is you can. You don't need an ecstatic experience. You don't need to discover a previously hidden secret. Just do what God told you to do. Get started, and He will be glorified. No magic required, just simple obedience.

Conclusion

Remember that piece of paper you folded in half? It is time to open it again. Look at the list of priorities you wrote on the left-hand side. Examine them. Are they actual priorities or aspirational priorities? Ask the Lord to reveal what your real priorities have been. List those on the right side of the paper. Don't rush. Be honest with yourself and with God.

Three questions will reveal your true priorities. Ask yourself:

1. How do I spend my time?
2. How do I use my talents?
3. How do I spend my treasures?

Where you spend your time, talents, and treasures reveals your true priorities. Jesus Himself said, "For where your treasure is, there your heart will be also" (Matt. 6:21).

Take some time to get alone with God and your piece of paper. Honestly compare your actual priorities with what you now understand to be God's priorities for your life. Ask the Lord to

- forgive you where you have let His priorities slip. He is always faithful to forgive and restore His children.
- help you get on track.
- adjust your priorities to align with His priorities for your life.

Trust Him to strengthen you, help you, and provide whatever you need to live out His priorities for your life. Gather the available resources, get to work, and glorify God!

And now comes the hard part.

Application

If you have not yet taken the test, do so now in the space below.

ASPIRATIONAL PRIORITIES	ACTUAL PRIORITIES

Chapter 2

Living Your Priorities

When I first saw him, I assumed he was an ambitious hotel manager, enhancing public relations. His smile was warm and welcoming. He chatted with guests at each table as he made his way around the dining area. Cindy, Ben, and I enjoyed our Sunday morning breakfast. He progressed guest-to-guest, table-to-table, toward a divine appointment with me. When he approached us, I realized he was a friendly guest rather than the manager. We were pleased when he asked to sit with us. He informed us he was in town for a motivational speaking engagement and asked what brought us to coastal New Hampshire.

"I'm here for a speaking engagement as well," I said.

He was good. He immediately turned the conversation toward our common interest in communication. His motivational specialty was life-priorities.

"Realize it or not," he said, "we all have priorities. We reveal them in how we spend our time, talents, and treasures. While I encourage people to list their priorities on paper, there's a bigger problem. Most never begin living them. My specialty is helping people live out their priorities."

I was intrigued. "How do you motivate people to move from having a priority list to actually living their priorities?"

"I teach them how to tap into the power that lies deep within each of us," he said. "We all possess the power to change. We all can live out our priorities. We just don't realize it."

Our new friend's problem diagnosis was spot on [living is more important than listing], but his prescription was a powerless placebo.

We'll circle back to the breakfast table in a bit. For now, let's turn our attention back to Jerusalem in Haggai's day.

Diagnosis

Twenty-three days had passed since Haggai's first sermon. The people could not get the message out of their minds. He had diagnosed their problem exactly. They knew Haggai was right.

> Jerusalem (536 BC)—God brought them back to the promised land from seventy years of exile in Babylon.
>   • *Their assignment.* Rebuild the temple.
>   • *The reason.* Levitical worship and sacrifice would instruct, bless, and prosper God's people once again.

They started the work soon after arriving. Problems, big problems, made the work difficult. Setbacks grew into major obstacles that appeared impossible to overcome. The work was put on hold indefinitely.

> Jerusalem (520 BC)—The temple remained in ruins.
>   • *Their problem.* Misplaced priorities. They aspired to please God, put Him first, and rebuild the temple. But aspirations did not transition into actions. Their actual priorities were different. They built their own houses and careers. God's priority assignment was neglected.
>   • *Their excuse.* "What more can we do? Times are tough. The climate has changed. Crops have failed. The econ-

omy is collapsing. We'd like to rebuild, but now isn't a good time" (1:2–5).

- *The reality*. No matter what their aspirations or excuses, their will, not God's, was first place in their lives.

The Lord confronted, corrected, and commanded them to adjust their priorities.

Twenty-three days passed. They still had done nothing but think about their problems. Even so, change was coming.

Prescription

God was gracious despite their procrastination. He sent Haggai to clarify His present judgement, which was the true cause of the adverse climate and crop failures (vv. 6, 9–11), and offer future deliverance. Repentance would renew God's favor and restore His blessings (vv. 7-8).

Twenty-three days after Haggai's first sermon (v. 15), the people responded. They "obeyed the voice of the LORD" (v. 12).

In light of the ancient Israelis' response to Haggai's diagnosis and prescription, allow me to ask the question I often ask myself, "Are you living God's priorities for your life?" I have discovered that an affirmative answer requires three substantial attitude adjustments.

Respect His Presence

First, I must *respect the Lord's presence*. Instead of ignoring the Lord, I must repent. Genuine repentance toward God engenders respect for God. I recognize His just chastening in my life.

So it happened in Jerusalem. Repentant people "feared the presence of the LORD" (v. 12). They changed a sixteen-year pattern.

For sixteen years, Jerusalem's residents kept the idea of rebuilding the temple on their aspirational priority list. Each year, however, it was bumped a little further down the list. They failed to make it an actual priority. They did not work on the temple.

Hearing Haggai's first sermon, however, was their "come to Yahweh moment." They repented; they respected the Lord's presence. With a sudden eye-opening flash, they realized, "God is watching how we spend our time, talents, and treasures. Even though we've ignored God's assignment, He hasn't ignored us. He disciplined us. He put a hole in our moneybags, sent a drought, and blew our crops away."

God was not cruel. He is the King and Lord. His will is primary, not secondary. His will is also the path to His blessings. He watched their actions and corrected their misplaced priorities. When they recognized God's chastening hand, they gained a new respect for His presence.

God Knows

Sinful habits, even sixteen-year patterns, can be broken. Isn't that encouraging?

The first step is realizing God is always with us. He sees and knows all we do.

Respecting His presence revolutionizes our choices. How? We realize He is available for personal consultation. We can consult Him about how to invest our time, use our talents, and spend our treasures. He's the only one who can mend the hole in our pockets and send refreshing rains, reviving the withered crops.

Haggai spoke God's revealed Word directly to God's people. He gave them God's diagnosis and prescription. Today we hear God's Word in our Bibles. God's written Word reveals His will about our time, talents, and treasures. His indwelling Spirit illuminates our understanding. Knowing His will, we can choose His priorities.

My Priority, Not Mom's

Mike, one of my older brothers, drove me to play in a junior varsity (JV) football game. I did not yet have my driver's license. The varsity team was playing immediately after my game, and we planned to stay. We wanted some cash for after the games.

Mike and I had a paper route together, and Mr. Billinger owed us some money. We decided to collect on the way to my game.

Mike kept the car running while I went to the door. When Mr. Billinger opened his door to pay me, his dog ran out.

The dog had a longstanding grudge against me. I threw papers at his master's house, and he did not like it. In fact, he considered it intolerable. Whenever I threw papers, he growled and snarled and barked as if he wanted to tear me apart. His master usually kept him inside or on a leash. But that day, he was free and fully intended to get revenge.

Before the owner realized what was happening, his dog attacked my knee. Mr. Billinger pulled his dog back into the house, apologizing profusely. I waved him off and hobbled back to the car.

"Are you okay?" Mike asked as I slammed the car door.

"No! It hurts!"

Mike drove into a nearby parking lot to take a closer look. He used the first aid kit we kept in the car to stop the bleeding, clean the wound, and bandaged my knee.

"What do you want to do?" he asked.

"What do you mean?"

"I should take you home and tell Mom what happened. I expect she'll send you to the doctor for stiches and a tetanus shot."

"But I'll miss my game."

"No doubt," Mike said. "It's your knee. I'll let you decide."

After a few moments of thought, I made a bad decision. "Mom doesn't know this happened," I said. "Even if she didn't send me to the doctor, she'd worry. And she wouldn't let me play football tonight. I want to play, so let's go to the game. We can keep this to ourselves."

So we did.

Needless to say, it wasn't my best day on the football field. I did the best I could with a chunk missing from my knee. It hurt a lot more than I expected, and it started bleeding again. The bandage needed changing often. That didn't help my play. When the coach realized what was happening, he sat me on the bench for the rest of the game.

After the JV game, I was in no hurry to go home. Mike and I stayed for the varsity game as planned. After the games, we went for burgers with some friends. Mike walked and I limped into the house several hours later.

Mom was waiting. "Where have you been?"

"At the game," I said, trying not to grimace.

Mike tried to look innocent.

"Are you all right, Mark?"

"Yeah, Mom. I didn't get hurt. You worry too much about football."

"Boys, I'm not talking about football! Mr. Billinger called."

"Oh."

"Let me see your leg."

Isn't it strange how moms seem to be omniscient about their children's lives? It is almost impossible to keep a secret from them. At least, that was the way it seemed with my mom. But again, I was a slow learner. Until that moment, it never dawned on me that Mom would know about the bad choices we made in the previous hours.

That night, my priority and Mom's clashed. My priority was playing football. Mom's priority was my well-being. She wanted what was best for me and my leg.

Mom didn't see the dog bite me. Mr. Billinger called, offering to pay my medical expenses. In the process, he revealed what I tried to hide.

Too often, God's people forget that we cannot hide anything from Him. Our Lord needs no calls. He sees all. He knows all. He is everywhere (Ps. 139:2–5, 7–12). He even knows the thoughts and intents of our hearts (Heb. 4:12).

God is omniscient and omnipresent. Realizing God knows everything and is always present everywhere, we can respect His presence. It is a necessary attitude adjustment as we move toward living out His priorities for our lives. Respecting His presence leads to a second substantial attitude adjustment.

Rely on His Promise

We can *rely on our Lord's promise*. "I am with you, says the LORD" (Hag. 1:13). Sometimes He corrects and sometimes He comforts, but He's always with us. He never promised living His priorities would be easy. He promised to be with us. "For He Himself has said, 'I will never leave you, nor forsake you'" (Heb. 13:5).

When the road is easy, He is with us. When the road is difficult, He's still with us. When we have all we need, He's with us. When resources evaporate, He's there. When we rely on His promise, we can stop worrying, trust Him, and get busy obeying. Remember David's words, "The LORD is my Shepherd, I shall not want" (Ps. 23:1). The promise of His presence empowers us to live according to His priorities.

> *Jerusalem* (520 BC)—The circumstances did not suddenly change for the people living in Jerusalem in Haggai's day. After his first sermon, they were still surrounded by enemies. Those enemies were still determined to prevent the temple's rebuilding. Their resources were still depleted. The economy had not improved. The drought continued. The little seed they had for planting was still in their barns. Their moneybags were not suddenly filled. They still had no visible hope of acquiring silver and gold to complete the temple.

Yet they had something better. They had the promise of their Lord's presence.

The same is true for you and me. If God is with us, there is no reason to worry. Our outward circumstances do not dictate our obedience. Outward circumstances do not compel us to abandon God's priorities for our lives. Circumstances do not limit God. They demonstrate our weakness and invite us to rely on His presence. In our weakness, He is strong.

> ➤ *Dallas* (1989)—Cindy and I had been married less than four years. We were working at a children's home in Dallas, Texas, and attending Criswell College. Our salary was not lucrative, but it was sufficient. We had no housing costs or grocery bills. In fact, our only living expenses were clothes and a car. We had good insurance and a retirement plan. The children's home provided both. Cindy and I each received a small paycheck at the end of each month. We were not getting rich, but our needs were met.

For several months, the Lord prepared us to leave the children's home. He was moving us toward my calling to pastor a church. Criswell College had a *ministry board*. Opportunities to serve in local churches were posted regularly.

Throughout the fall semester, I checked the board almost daily. Nothing seemed to fit us, but I continued to check. Though initially I ignored it, one listing repeatedly drew my attention.

A church in North Dallas was looking for several couples to plant churches out of their congregation. It sounded interesting, but it included numerous challenges.

I wanted a safer option. I wanted to pastor an established church. Yet, the listing kept grabbing my attention. Each time I read it, the last line "Compensation: $200 a month" screamed, "RUN AWAY!"

One day, Cindy went to school with me. While I took a final exam, she visited the *ministry board*. When my test was over, Cindy met me in the hall. "Mark, we have been praying for an opportunity to lead a church. I just read an interesting item on the ministry board."

Somehow I knew what she had seen.

"No!" I said. "We can't do it. Did you see the compensation?"

Cindy heard my adamant attitude. She left it in God's hands and said no more.

Fifteen minutes later, we merged onto I-30, heading home. The ride had been silent up to that point. Suddenly, I merged back off the highway.

"What are you doing?"

"Going back to get the number for that church planting opportunity."

She just smiled.

Things moved quickly. Within a week, we faced a major decision. Somehow we sensed that the way we dealt with this choice would set a pattern for our lives. Would we seek the Lord's direction, or would we automatically rule out an option that lacked sufficient resources?

Within a very short time, we understood the Lord was calling us to leave our comfort zone, step out in faith, and start a new congregation. We had no idea how we would make it, but we chose to trust His presence to be sufficient.

The next few years were not easy. Many days, we did not know how we could continue. One day, we had no food and no money to buy food. We prayed. We relied on His presence. Before the day ended, He provided in an astounding way.

We learned a lesson that has lasted a lifetime. We can respect God's presence and rely on His promises. He is sufficient. With His help, we can live out His priorities for our lives.

Respond to His Promptings

A third substantial adjustment has helped me live God's priorities for my life. This is where shoe leather is applied—adjusting attitudes leads to adjusted actions. We can *respond to the Lord's promptings.*

Adjustment in Jerusalem

The saga in Jerusalem continued. "So the LORD stirred up the spirit of all the remnant of the people; and they came and worked on the house of the Lord of hosts, their God" (Hag 1:14).

Respecting His presence and relying on His promises prepared them to respond to His prompting.

For sixteen years, God called the Jerusalem residents to His work. This time they heard. This time they went to work. The Lord *stirred up their spirit*, and they responded with action. How about you? Has the Lord ever stirred your spirit?

The Lord may prompt you to share the Gospel, give a tract, or pray for a need. He may prompt you to give a sacrificial offering for His work or accept a new ministry role. When the Lord prompts, you must make a decision. Will you ignore or obey?

My advice, to borrow a popular phrase, is "Just do it!" Obey the Lord's promptings and you will live out His priorities.

Practicing His Priorities

On a recent business trip for both our denomination and for Northeastern Baptist College, I flew out of Albany, New York. Before boarding, I noticed a man with a walking cast on his right foot. The Lord prompted me to pray for him, so I offered a quick prayer for his physical and spiritual health.

After settling into my seat, I opened an app on my phone to select a book to read on the flight to Atlanta. I was about to begin when a man sat down next to me. You guessed it. It was the man with the walking cast. I was looking forward to reading my new book, but the Lord prompted me to begin a conversation.

Within seconds, the man began telling me about his foot. I expressed concern, and he began telling his life story. I knew more about him before the plane took off than I expected to learn on the entire two-hour flight.

The conversation moved forward from discussing his physical health to discussing his spiritual health. As I began to witness to him, my new friend interrupted.

"I know what you are going to ask," he said. "Yes, I am a believer. I was saved when I was a young." He described his family's faithful church attendance as he grew up, how he became a Christian, and how he had spent most of his adult life serving the Lord as a deacon in his church. The next thing he said surprised me. "I've been running from God for the last five years."

We talked about the events that led him to run from God and walk away from church. "I'm not afraid to die," he said. "If this plane crashed right now, I know where I would go. I'd go straight to heaven. No, I'm not afraid to die. I'm ashamed to die. In fact, that's why I don't go back to church. I'm too ashamed to face the people."

Before the flight ended, my new friend considered returning to the Lord and to his church family. Tears were in his eyes as we talked about the prodigal son returning home. We exchanged cell numbers, and at the time I am writing this our periodic texting continues.

Obedience to one prompting led to another prompting. Obeying the second prompting opened an opportunity to influence a fellow believer's life. Responding to God's prompting allowed me to live out one of His priorities for my life, encouraging believers to faithfully walk with God.

The same will be true in your life. If you respect the Lord's presence, rely on His promises, and respond in obedience to His promptings, you will live out His priorities for your life. How are you doing with your priorities?

Back to Breakfast

The motivational speaker finished his story and asked about my specialty.

"I speak about living your priorities as well," I said. "I agree with your diagnosis, but I disagree with your prescription. We need internal power, but I don't believe everyone has a power within to release."

He was surprised. "Where would we get the power to change?" he asked.

"From God," I said.

"Oh, sure," he said. "The power within is God. Don't you believe God is in everyone?"

"Do you believe God was in Hitler?" I asked.

"Hmm, no. I guess not."

"Then God isn't within everyone. Yet everyone can have Him within. We are talking about different things. You think God must be released. I believe He must be received." And I stepped through the door God opened. With joy, I lived one of my life-priorities—sharing the gospel with unbelievers. I gave a clear, simple gospel presentation and invited my new friend to receive Jesus Christ into his life.

He didn't respond that day, but as he left with my phone number, he said, "This is very interesting. You've given me a lot to think about."

Because of His presence, promise, and prompting, I was able to live out one of God's priorities for my life at a breakfast table in New Hampshire. You, too, can live out God's priorities wherever you are. The amazing bonus: God will "take pleasure in it and be glorified" (Hag. 1:8).

Respect His presence. Rely on His promise. Respond to His promptings. Live God's priorities for your life.

Application

Attitude Assessment: Chuck Swindoll often says, "Life is 90% attitude and 10% what happens to you." Whether things are going well or trials abound, your attitude influences your actions.

Take a few minutes to reflect on chapter 2, "Living Your Priorities." Consider the following questions:

1. How does my attitude impact my actions in living out God's priorities for my life?
2. How does the fact that God knows my every word, thought, and deed impact my attitude about living out His priorities for my life?
3. How do God's promises impact my attitude and actions in regard to living out His priorities?
4. How quickly and completely do I respond to the Holy Spirit's promptings in my life?
5. What specific things do I need to do to adjust my attitude today?

Chapter 3

Continuing in Your Priorities

White noises—the sounds we uncon-sciously tune out, background noise we ignore. What we hear but don't hear. For most, ocean wave sounds, birds chirping, and oscillating fans qualify as white noises.

For me, radio commercials are usually white noise, especially when I'm driving. I tune them out. That's why a few years back, a commercial surprised me. It grabbed my attention. Instead of selling a product, the attention grabber offered to buy, and the offer was sincere.

"How are your New Year's resolutions working out?" the announcer began. "Is that expensive gym equipment just sitting in your bedroom, living room, or garage? Bring it to "Play It Again Sports." We'll buy your lightly used New Year's resolution!"

The company profits from a familiar cycle. Maybe you recognize it.

- December—Treadmill, stationary bike, or weight lifting equipment purchased at an *after Christmas sale*.
- January (New Year's Resolution)—Workout five days a week, one hour per day. Begin low carb diet. Trim down; tone up. Beach body by June.
- Mid-January—Daily workouts losing their charm. Workout changes to three days a week, thirty minutes a day. Craving carbs. Beach vacation reservations made.
- February—Workout on hold while recovering from exercise injury. Low carb diet postponed until after Super Bowl party.
- March—Sports equipment in bedroom is now expensive but convenient coat rack.
- April—New Year's resolution drifts to bottom of priority list.
- May—Beach vacation canceled.
- June—Buyer's remorse sets in; unneeded coat rack moved to garage.
- November—Finding source for extra Christmas cash moves to top of priority list.

- December—Borrow brother-in-law's pickup to haul expensive exercise equipment to "Play It Again Sports."

The company buys at a discount and resells at a profit. One's source of Christmas cash becomes another's Christmas present or New Year's resolution. And so, the cycle continues.

I thought, *Brilliant! I wish I had thought of that.*

From another perspective, however, it's sad. Many never evaluate their priorities. Of those who do, relatively few adjust their lives to actually live their priorities. Of those who make the adjustment, all struggle to continue living out the priorities past the first few weeks.

Assignment Revisited

We prayed and made a priority list based on our present understanding of God's priorities for our lives. With His help and relying on the principles we learned in the last chapter, we can adjust our lives. We can begin living God's priorities. But as with a workout and diet, beginning is not enough. As time passes, challenges increase. Initial passion wanes.

"Play It Again Sports" is not alone in understanding human nature. God "knows our frame; He remembers that we *are* dust" (Ps. 103:14).

How can we stay on track and continue living God's priorities?

Return to Jerusalem

Less than a month had passed since the Jerusalem residents restarted the temple restoration and rebuilding project, the Father was well aware the workmen were weary. The task was large. The challenges were many. The resources were few.

Understanding their frailty, God sent Haggai to preach his second sermon. The sermon's purpose was to encourage the Lord's people to stay the course. It was crucial that God's people not abandon His priorities. They must not revert to pursuing their own comforts. They must press forward and complete their assignment.

The Father gave them three principles to enable them to continue living His priorities. These same three principles can help you continue to live out God's priorities for your life.

Remember the Past

Haggai asked three questions at the beginning of his second sermon.

- *"Who is left among you who saw this temple in its former glory?"* Some of the people had been alive when the nation was taken into captivity eighty-six years earlier. A few had been old enough to remember the temple's glory.

- *"And how do you see it now?"* A month into the work and they were still clearing the work site. The once magnificent temple was nothing but an overwhelming heap of crumbling stones and debris.
- *"In comparison with it, is this not in your eyes as nothing?"* Didn't Haggai intend to encourage the workers? If so, why the discouraging words? Why remind them of their past glory and their present gloom? Was Haggai sabotaging his own sermon?

Haggai wanted the people to remember the past and be realistic about the present. If we refuse to look at our present realistically, we may accept it as inevitable. "I don't like it," we say, "but I can't change it. I might as well accept it and try to be satisfied." If, however, we recognize our current reality is not inevitable, we can envision a better future.

The people in Jerusalem needed to remember the temple's glory as a motivation to keep working. Rather than mourning the devastation, they could be motivated to rebuild.

"If God did that through Solomon, He can do it again through us!" The same is true for you and me today.

The Northeast was once the Bible Belt of America. The first Baptists in America founded Rhode Island.

The influence of Rhode Island Baptists paved the way for religious freedom in the United States.

William Screven started the first Baptist church in the South when he led his congregation from the Maine/New Hampshire state line to South Carolina to begin a new church.

This is the land of the Great Awakenings. It is the land of the haystack prayer meeting that sparked the American Missionary Movement. It is the birthplace of Adoniram Judson, Luther Rice, and Dwight L. Moody.

Today the Northeast includes the least churched states in America. Consider Vermont.

At one time, most Vermont towns had a congregational church and a Baptist church. There were enough Baptists in Vermont to support a Vermont Baptist historical society until 1924.

Today the church buildings are still there, but many are no longer functioning churches. The buildings are now town offices, antique shops, restaurants, or judo schools.

Town after town in Vermont has no gospel witness. Approximately, 2 percent of the population in most Vermont counties claim to have a relationship with Jesus Christ; three counties are exceptional. About 3.5 percent claim to know Jesus. By the standards of most international mission agencies, Vermont is *an unreached* if not *unengaged* people group. The spiritual climate is similar in most of the New England and Northeastern states.

At Northeastern Baptist College, we have found it is crucial to *remember the past*. God used Roger Williams to make a difference in Rhode Island. God used William Screven to make a difference in Maine and South Carolina. God used Jonathan Edwards, George Whitfield, and D. L. Moody to make a difference in Massachusetts and many other regions. If God used them, despite their challenging circumstances, overt opposition, and lack of resources, He can use us. NEBC can make a difference today.

Likewise, your church can make a difference today. You can make a difference today. Remember what God has done through His people in the past; it will encourage you to live out His priorities for your life in the present.

D. L. Moody admired Charles Haddon Spurgeon. On his first trip to England, Moody was determined to see Spurgeon and hear him preach. Though he was told he could not be admitted because of the crowds, Moody persisted until he was able to hear Spurgeon. The two men met and became great friends. Moody read anything Spurgeon wrote and was strongly influenced by him.

Moody once remarked, "Spurgeon did not accomplish so much because He was a great man, but because He served a great God." Moody saw how God used Spurgeon. Instead of being intimidated, he was inspired. If God can accomplish great things through Spurgeon, Moody thought, *He can use me too*.

When you feel yourself wanting to let go of God's priorities in your life...

- Remember the past. Reflect on how God has used others before you. God carried them through despite challenges, opposition, and a lack of resources.
- Remember ways God has used you in the past. Renew your determination to obey God. Renew your focus on living out the Lord's priorities for your life.
- Trust God to deal with your challenges, opposition, and lack of resources.
- Press on!

Rely on His Presence

God understood the Jews' fearful circumstances. The Lord commanded Zerubbabel the governor, Joshua the high priest, and all the people, "Be strong...do not fear!" (Hag. 2:4, 5).

Many have noted that "do not fear" is God's most often repeated Bible command. They say it is found 366 times, once for each day of the year and an extra for leap year. I'm not 100 percent certain about that. I haven't counted them. But I am certain that fear often strikes, and Christians are not exempt.

Fear is an ever-present obstacle along the path of living out God's priorities. We fear people. We fear disappointing our friends. We fear criticism and condemnation from the devil and his crew. But whether the fear comes from a friend or a foe, "The fear of man lays a snare" (Prov. 29:25, ESV). Don't step in the fear trap.

God's priorities seldom match the trends of the times. It can be frightening to realize God has called you to go against the flow. None of us enjoy unpopularity. We don't want to rub people the wrong way. We don't want to appear to hinder progress. But that often happens to those following the path of God's priorities. Along the way, we may feel alone and abandoned.

Feeling Discouraged?

If you are feeling discouraged, stay with me. There's hope ahead. I promise.

We are dealing with reality realistically. We are not creating "Christian-hype." No false advertising here.

The Problem

The path of God's priorities is a part of the *narrow way*. Jesus described His path as the "narrow way," and the world's path as "the wide way." The narrow way is not popular. It rubs many people the wrong way. It appears its travelers are hindering progress. After all, the narrow way inconveniently is in the middle of the wide way, but the narrow way's traffic pattern is uphill in the opposite direction.

Jesus said, "Enter by the narrow gate; for wide *is* the gate and broad *is* the way that leads to destruction, and there are many who go in by it. Because narrow *is* the gate and difficult *is* the way which leads to life, and there are few who find it" (Matt. 7:13–14).

Why would anyone want to join the few on a narrow, difficult, unpopular road? Your answer depends on your desired destination. The wide road leads to destruction. The narrow road leads to life. The enemy does all he can to frighten folks away from the narrow gate.

We who have received Jesus Christ as our Savior are on the way, but we haven't arrived. Our destination is still in the distance. When we get there, we'll be mighty glad we chose this path.

Despite the enemy's activities, he can't get us off the narrow way. Our salvation is secure. But he wants to make us ineffective in our service on the narrow way. That's why he does all he can to derail us on the path of God's priorities. He wants to make us an obstacle for others.

Fear distracts, discourages, and derails; the enemy knows it. We threaten the enemy when we begin daily living out God's priorities. Therefore, he wants us to be fearful. He wants us to abandon the path the Lord led us to follow. Spiritual opposition is part of the uncomfortable news.

I Am with You

Yet there is comforting news. Since God knows fear is debilitating, He provided the remedy. Between His two commands "be strong" (Hag. 2:4) and "do not fear" (v. 5), God stated the reason His children can obey both: "For I am with you!" The remedy for fear is recognizing God's personal presence.

When the work is hard, "I am with you." When resources are depleted, "I am with you." When the land faces a drought, "I am with you." When enemies want to destroy you, "I am with you." God gives strength in our weaknesses. He provides for our needs even when our resources are gone. God feeds us even in the midst of a drought. No enemy is stronger than our God. If He is with us, no one can ultimately stand against us.

David, the sweet psalmist of Israel, noted, "Yea, though I walk through the valley of the shadow of death, I will fear no evil for You are with me!"

God's presence enables His people to press forward even in the face of fear.

A Walk in the Dark

I grew up in Colorado. Each fall, the men and boys in my family spent a few weeks in the mountains, camping and hunting elk and mule deer. Dad began to let me go when I was eight years old.

My second hunting season, our deer harvest was divided into two separate weeks. Dad, my oldest brother Jim, and I went during the September muzzle-loading season. Later in November, we deer hunted a second week with regular rifles. After a few days of the September hunt, we found a place where a deer herd bedded down each night. No matter how early we got there, somehow we missed them.

One afternoon, we split up. Jim went one direction; Dad and I went another. We planned to meet up just after dark. By the end of the day, however, Dad and I were back at the *bedding down* spot. Dad suggested we spend the night in a tree. At dawn, we would be right above the herd and could harvest the choice ones.

"What do you think?" Dad asked.

To a nine-year-old boy, a night in a tree sounded great, a fun adventure.

"Let's do it!" I said. If Tarzan and my dad could do it, so could I.

We climbed a tree. I picked a limb for a bed. Dad did the same. Even on a tree limb, weariness from the long day of hiking enveloped me. Within minutes, I was unconscious.

It seemed only a minute had passed when my dad's whispered call woke me. "Mark. Mark. Wake up. I'm getting too old for this. Let's go to camp."

It was 2:00 a.m. I had slept nearly five hours on that limb.

We climbed down, crossed an open area, and started through the heavily wooded forest. It was a starless night. Within five minutes, we were deep in the woods.

Dad reached back and grabbed me. "Mark," he said, "grab onto my coattail. Don't let go. It's too dark to see. You must hold on."

As we continued deeper into the woods, even though he was right in front of me, I could no longer see him. *I could not see my hand in front of my face.* That was an uncomfortable fact, not a cliché. So I did what Dad told me to do. I held on to his coattail; I did not let go.

From time to time, Dad said, "Let's stop for a minute."

He clicked a lighter on, using the flame's light to examine the ground around us. Then we moved on. Eventually, we heard my brother Jim honking the truck horn. Soon we heard him yelling. Dad followed the sound until we saw the truck lights. We followed the light to our destination.

Much of the journey from the tree to the truck was in total darkness. As I followed blindly clutching Dad's coattail, I thought, *What if we run across a grizzly bear or a mountain lion?* Sometimes I was afraid we were lost for good. But I was only a little concerned. I knew Dad knew the woods. He was tough. He fought in World War II in much worse conditions. He was big. He was strong. He had a gun. He loved me. He would care for me. I might not know where I was or how we were going to get through, but Dad was with me. All I had to do was obey his command: "Hold onto my coattail. Don't let go." I was safe because he was with me.

Eventually, I learned that as big and as strong as my dad was sometimes even he didn't know what to do. At times, he didn't know how he would make it. Dad was limited.

Our heavenly Father, in contrast, is unlimited. He knows all. He sees all. He has all power and authority. His resources are never depleted. No one can stand against Him. He was with the Jews in Jerusalem despite the opposition they faced. They could continue to live out God's priorities for their lives no matter what their challenges were.

The same is true for you. You can continue to live out God's priorities for your life no matter the opposition or challenge. He has promised to be with you; He will never leave you. Be strong. Do not fear. Live His priorities for your life.

Rest in His Promises

When you feel like giving up on God's priorities, *remember the past, rely on His presence,* and *rest in His promises.*

During the time I pastored in Virginia, Promise Keepers, a popular men's movement, arose. Several Christian leaders were involved in the movement. The movement's initiators recognized a major problem in our country. Many men had abandoned the idea of keeping their promises. This left a void of faithful male leadership in the home, the church, and the community.

The movement took two major forms:

- First, large events in sports arenas and stadiums brought Christian and non-Christian men together. Enthusiastic contemporary Christian music and dynamic speakers challenged men to trust Jesus for salvation, live under His Lordship, and become faithful *promise keepers*.
- Second, men were encouraged to start small groups focused on encouraging one another to keep seven key promises that would have an impact at home, at church, and in the community.

The movement had a great aim. It made a positive impact on many men and churches. Men certainly should keep their promises. Over the years, however, I observed three things about being a promise keeper. First, some people never intend to keep promises. This is a major problem the movement confronted. Second, sometimes we want to keep our promises, but we fail despite our best attempts. Third, sometimes we do everything within our power to keep a promise but circumstances beyond our control thwart us. We have neither the power nor the resources to keep a promise.

True Promise Keeper

We should strive to keep our promises, but there is only one true promise keeper. "Heaven and earth will pass away," said Jesus, "but My words will by no means pass away" (Matt. 24:35). Jesus keeps His promises.

Consider three encouraging assurances.

- First, Jesus Christ's deity dictates that He cannot lie. The apostle Paul declared this fact in light of a promise. He spoke of the "hope of eternal life which God, who cannot lie, promised before time began" (Titus 1:2). He will never mislead us; God keeps His promises.
- Second, Jesus always does what He intends to do. No one can thwart His good intentions. "But our God *is* in heaven; He does whatever He pleases" (Ps. 115:3). Aren't you glad He is pleased to keep His promises?
- Third, no circumstance or power in all of creation can stop Jesus from keeping His promises. He is all-powerful and all good.

Therefore, He will *always* keep His promises! Not only can we *rely on His presence*, we can *rest in His promises*.

Trustworthy Promises

The same was true in Haggai's day. His second sermon to the people living in Jerusalem called them to continue living out their priorities based on God's three inspiring promises.

- *God's Power.* First, we have the promise of God's power. God said through Haggai, "Once more, I will shake heaven and earth...I will shake all nations, and they shall come to the Desire of All Nations, and I will fill this Temple with glory" (2:6–7).

  When Haggai proclaimed his message, his enemies surrounding Jerusalem were working to shut down the temple rebuilding project permanently. The temple site was in ruins. The work was receiving their attention for the first time in sixteen years. The project's future looked bleak, if not impossible, yet God's promises gave them hope. God's enemies are no match for God's power. He will complete His plans; no one can stop Him.

  God's people face opposition. Nothing is new or unique about it. Yet "He who is in you is greater than he who is in the world" (1 John 4:4). Live God's priorities, resting in His promised power.

- *God's Provision.* Second, we can rest in God's promised provision. Haggai continued, "'The silver is Mine, and the gold is Mine,' says the LORD of hosts" (2:8). Why mention this fact?

The Jews lacked money and materials to build the temple. They could get wood from the Mount of Olives (1:8), but they needed more than wood. Solomon's Temple was overlaid with gold and silver. They had none, so Haggai exhorted them to rest in God's promised provision. They began clearing the rubble and ruins from the Temple Mount in faith.

God owns everything, whether we know it or not. He said, "The silver is Mine, and the gold is Mine." King Darius thought he owned it. In reality, God had only temporarily entrusted a few riches into Darius's control.

In effect, God said, "I own everything and I have promised to provide for you. You may not have it now. You may not know where to get it. Your circumstances look bleak. Just trust and obey. I will provide when the time is right."

The same is true for you and me.

As we begin living by God's priorities, challenges often increase. We wonder how we will make it. Our circumstances discourage us, but God says, "Trust and obey! Follow Me! Live out My priorities for your life. Your resources may be gone, but My resources are unlimited. Trust me. Rest in My provision. Don't quit!"

- *God's Pictured Future.* God promised a glorious future for the restored temple. Picture it.

  "'The glory of this latter temple shall be greater than the former,' says the LORD of hosts. 'And in this place, I will give peace,' says the LORD of hosts" (2:9).

  With God's promises, your future is bright. It will look much different than your current circumstances. What He will do is built on what you do now. Live His priorities now. You will be a part of the glorious future He promises. The result will be great!

  Someday all nations will fill the temple. Why? They will come to "the desire of all nations" (v. 7). They will see "the glory" and experience the promised "peace" (v. 9). Notice a multilayered meaning. Each is glorious.

Near Meaning

The near meaning is *impersonal.* Several contemporary translations, such as the English Standard Version, emphasize this fact. "'And I will shake all nations, so that *the treasures of all nations shall come in*, and I will fill this house with glory,' says the Lord of hosts."

The wealth to complete the temple will come from the nations. And so, it did. Eventually, Herod used Roman tax money to enlarge the Temple Mount and cover the temple's interior with gold. Herod boasted that he had outdone Solomon. Remember, he refurbished the temple the Jews finally completed in Haggai's day. God's promise will be fulfilled even if it takes five hundred years to do it.

Distant Meaning

The distant meaning is *personal*. "The Desire of All Nations" is the coming Messiah, Jesus Christ. Jesus entered Herod's Temple, and crowds flocked to see Him. Further, a Messianic Temple will be rebuilt on the Temple Mount following Jesus's second coming to earth. From His Jerusalem Temple, He will personally rule over the earthly Millennial Kingdom.

Is the pictured future possible? For most, "the Desire of All Nations" is not a present reality. The opposite is true. Most nations are either indifferent or hostile toward Jesus. That will change. Someday every knee will bow before the Lord Jesus. Every tongue will confess that Jesus Christ is Lord (Phil. 2:9–11).

Is the pictured future personal for you? Have you confessed "Jesus is my Lord"? Don't wait. You can live under Jesus's loving Lordship now.

The final confession described in Philippians 2 will be forced. It will be a precursor to eternal condemnation. And by the way, you don't want to be in that crowd.

Ancient-Contemporary Meaning

In considering the multilayered meaning, don't lose sight of Haggai's encouragement for his contemporaries. When Haggai spoke, none of it seemed possible. The temple was in ruins. Their enemies were resisting. Their resources were depleted. In light of the bleak situation, Haggai exhorted them to believe God's promises. Trust God's power, God's provisions, and God's picture of the future.

Haggai Helped Me

It was the most intense week I have faced in ministry. The Lord was blessing NEBC's work. Through the ministries of our students, staff, and faculty, unprecedented numbers of people had recently trusted Jesus. Even so, our financial challenges seemed insurmountable. Anticipated donations were not given. Nothing came in to replace our depleted resources.

In addition, opposition abounded. I cannot count the number of times someone in our NEBC family contacted me with a major challenge. The college was under spiritual attack.

My family was not exempt. We faced numerous health challenges on both Cindy's side of the family and mine.

Calls came in from pastors, churches, and church members. All were facing opposition that threatened to derail them from impacting the Northeast with the Gospel. It was intense!

That week, I spent a lot of time reading scripture and praying. As the Lord helped me get perspective on one problem, another challenge hit me. The week progressed and the battle intensified. I tried to encourage myself in the Lord. "We do not wrestle against flesh and blood," I reminded myself. "I must put on God's full armor. I will be victorious." I continued my work, but the battle took its toll.

"Mark," I asked myself, "is all this worth it?" A series of thoughts pointed to a negative conclusion. "Look at your battles. You brought this attack on yourself and your family. And what about your faculty and staff? They had good jobs. Why did you ask them to quit and join you? They would have been much better off staying where they were. You have made their lives difficult. And what about the students? Because of you, they are sinking in the same boat. Don't you see what you have done? All of it is your fault! What made you think you could start a Baptist college in the least churched state in America?"

Mark, why don't you just quit? The next series of thoughts pointed to a positive conclusion. *If you would simply admit that the battle is too hard, you could quit. You gave it a good shot. The challenges are too great, the opposition is too strong, and the resources are too few. Everyone sees it. No one will blame you for quitting. You could move on with your life. More importantly, if you will just call it quits, your family, faculty, staff, and students can move on. Their lives will be much easier.*

This all led to one final blow. *Mark, just give up your priorities. Everything would be much easier on everyone.*

Under the barrage, how could I continue living my present priorities? Were they really God's priorities for my life? Had I misunderstood?

I called out to the Lord. "I'm weak. I need Your strength."

He heard my prayer. He directed me to Psalm 43:5, "Why are you cast down, O my soul? And why are you disquieted within me? Hope in God; for I shall yet praise Him. The help of my countenance and my God."

I read it over and over. I prayed those words almost continually. Then the Lord brought me back to Haggai.

How do you continue to live out God's priorities for your life when the challenges are great, the opposition is strong, and the resources are depleted?

You remember the past! God has done great things before. He can do it again.

You rely on His presence! He Himself has promised, "I will never leave you nor forsake you."

You rest in His promises! He is all-powerful. Nothing can stop Him. He owns everything, and He will provide. He has a better future planned than you can possibly imagine. You just don't see it at the moment.

Fear gave way to faith. Faith gave way to action. Action led me to press forward, trusting and obeying. At NEBC, we not only teach our students to have the mind

DR. MARK H. BALLARD

of a scholar and the heart of a shepherd, but we also teach them to have the perseverance of a soldier. What we teach, we must demonstrate.

You too can persevere like a soldier. You can continue to live out God's priorities for your life. When it appears, you cannot take another step.

- Remember the past.
- Rely on His presence.
- Rest in His promises.

And who knows? If you adopt a soldier's perseverance mindset, maybe, just maybe, you won't need to borrow your brother-in-law's pickup truck next December.

Application

Take a few minutes to reflect on your own journey by answering the following questions.

1. What are the three biggest challenges you face today that threaten to distract, discourage, and derail you from continuing to live out God's priorities for your life?
2. Briefly describe a time you trusted God when you didn't know how you would make it, and He brought you through.
3. How can God's constant presence enable you to continue living out His priorities?
4. What are three specific promises from God's Word that you can hold onto when you feel like giving up?

Chapter 4

The Blessing of Living Your Priorities

Part 1

"God bless you!" If I hear it in public, at least in the Northeast, I wonder, "Who sneezed?"

Does "God bless you" mean anything more than "I hope you're not getting sick" or "Good luck"?

Are *happy happenings* always evidence of God's blessing? Are difficulties always evidence He is withholding His blessings? After a Super Bowl or a national championship game, you would think so.

It is common for one or more from the winning team to *thank the good Lord* for blessing them. They got to play and win the big game. We seldom hear it from anyone on the losing team.

Do God's blessings exempt us from problems, challenges, and trials? Do they guarantee health, wealth, and happiness?

The Bible teaches that God's people are blessed when they live His priorities for their lives. We are blessed whether our circumstances bring trials or triumphs, sickness or health, dwindling resources or wealth. God's people experience His blessings when we pursue God's priorities. But to be candid, His blessings do often include some physical and financial benefits. They did for the people in Jerusalem. But prosperity and ease are not guaranteed.

We can learn to think biblically about God's blessings. Haggai helped his neighbors in Jerusalem adjust their thinking and their priorities. In his third sermon, Haggai announced that God's blessings had come upon the people. God said, "From this day, I will bless you" (2:19).

What an exciting moment!

The people had labored for themselves, ignored God's priorities, and suffered under God's discipline. Then they heard Haggai's first sermon. They realized he was speaking God's Word, not his personal whim. They repented and began to live God's priorities for their lives. They began working on the temple again.

As previously noted, God gave an assignment when they returned from Babylon sixteen years earlier. He directed them to rebuild the temple. They began when they first returned, but they had serious problems and challenges. Quitting was easier than continuing, so they quit. They moved on to other personal priorities.

After restarting the work on the Temple Mount (1:14) and working hard for a month, the progress was slow. Again, they were tempted to quit. They may have thought, "If we're doing God's will, it shouldn't be this hard. Maybe we misunderstood."

God knew their thoughts. He understood and cared. He sent Haggai to encourage them with his second sermon—continue to live out God's priorities.

Don't quit even though it is difficult, which brings us to the third sermon.

Haggai announced God's blessing in response to their obedience. In announcing the new season of blessing, Haggai taught three key truths about God's blessings. Likely, these surprised the prophet's hearers. They may surprise you as well. If we are to think biblically about God's blessing, understanding what Haggai communicated is crucial.

Disguised Blessings

Do you wish you could forget certain parts of your past? When God forgives, He removes our sin as far as the east is from the west (Ps. 103:12). Paul said, "If anyone *is* in Christ, *he is* a new creation; old things have passed away; behold, all things have become new" (2 Cor. 5:17). He also said, "Forgetting those things which are behind and reaching forward to those things which are ahead, I press toward the goal for the prize of the upward call of God in Christ Jesus" (Phil. 3:13–14).

If those verses are true, why do we remember our past sins? If we are forgiven, if we are new creations now experiencing God's blessings, why can't we forget our past failures?

Haggai's third sermon (Hag. 2:10–19) reminded the Jews of their sinful past, God's discipline, and promised God's present blessings. On their own, they were defiled, corrupt, and sinful (vv. 10–14). The LORD described them, "Every work of their hands; and what they offer there is unclean" (v. 14). Don't miss an important truth: *God's present blessing does not erase our past.*

Haggai noted God's discipline. "'Since those *days,* when *one* came to a heap of twenty ephahs, there were *but* ten; when *one* came to the wine vat to draw out fifty baths from the press, there were *but* twenty. I struck you with blight and mildew and hail in all the labors of your hands; yet you did not *turn* to Me,' says the Lord" (vv. 16–17). God's blessings were real, but God's blessings did not erase their past.

God's discipline led them to repentance. They acknowledged their sin and turned away from it. God forgave them, and they adjusted their lives. They turned away from their own priorities and began living out God's priorities. They were working on the temple and were now candidates for God's supernatural favor.

God forgives and cleanses our sin. He redeems our past. We should be glad, however, that He does not erase our past. Remembering our past sins and God's chastening is a blessing in disguise.

Someone said, "Those who do not remember the past are doomed to repeat it." God does not want us to dwell on the past. He does not want us to be depressed by our past. He wants us to learn from our past. When we learn from our past, it helps us pursue His priorities in the present.

Crisis of Belief

Three days after surrendering to the Lord to start Northeastern Baptist College in Bennington, Vermont, I faced a crisis of belief.

On the morning of October 28, 2009, Cindy, Ben, and I picked up my sister Sherrill and her husband, Harvey. We headed to Northfield, Massachusetts to visit D. L. Moody's gravesite. On the way, we told Harvey and Sherrill what the Lord called us to do.

Near Northfield, I said, "We have come here to pray. Three out of four schools Moody started have turned away from the Bible and abandoned the Gospel message. I want us to pray that Northeastern Baptist College will never turn away from the truth."

We parked our vehicle and walked up the hill to Moody's grave. As we walked toward the grave marker, the coming financial struggle overwhelmed me. The weight on my shoulders seemed heavier with each step. We stood before Moody's grave for a moment. I told

Cindy, "I can't pray. You stay here with Sherrill and Harvey. Ben and I are going for a walk."

We found a park bench and sat down.

"Lord, I can't do this!" I prayed. "Father, how can I be a good dad to Benjamin and step out in faith with no hope of a salary to provide for his needs? Lord, Cindy and I have sacrificed repeatedly. We've gone to little or no salary to serve you. But things are different now. We have Ben. He has a lot of special needs. Lord, you know that. You gave him to us. How can I possibly make a move like this?"

Remember my story in chapter 1 about God's call to start a church in Florida? Our North Carolina church offered us a leave of absence. I knew in my heart that we should not worry about the future. We should trust God and obey His leading. Instead, I gave in to fear. Just before our return to North Carolina, the Lord showed us that He knew our needs. He had been working to prepare a place of service at the end of the summer. However, we missed the blessing of walking by faith. When we returned to North Carolina, the people we loved welcomed us. On the outside, we picked up where we left off in the spring. Inside, the Lord confronted, corrected, and chastened me.

God did not erase my 1994 failure from my mind. It flooded back into my mind on that park bench in Northfield.

It is never fruitful to run from God's leading in fear. I called out to the Lord, "I don't want to back away from Your call. I want to walk by faith, but I am weak." Honest confessions never surprise God.

Again, I asked, "Lord, how can I be a good dad to Ben and step out in faith with no salary?"

Immediately, I knew the answer. It was in the form of a question. "Mark, do you really think you love Benjamin more than I do?" The door to my fear dungeon unlocked and swung open.

The crisis of belief was over. We rejoined Cindy, Sherrill, and Harvey. After we prayed, I looked up and said, "Let's go start a college!"

If my failures and God's discipline in 1994 had been erased from memory, I might have walked away from God's call. The memory of those days was a blessing in disguise. That memory kept me on the bench, praying, seeking the Lord, and looking to Him for the strength to take the biggest step of faith in our lives.

God's blessing does not erase our past. Praise the Lord! Being reminded of our past failures at the right time and in the right way is a blessing in disguise. The reminder keeps us pressing forward, living out God's priorities.

Delayed Blessings

In our preaching classes at Northeastern Baptist College, we teach that a good sermon communicates the main theme of the text. When one discovers a text's true theme, the main points of the passage will support that theme. If a preacher does not communicate anything else, his listeners should remember the main theme of the passage.

Previously we noted the main theme of Haggai's third sermon: *God blesses His people for adjusting their lives to His priorities.*

Imagine you are a Jew living in Jerusalem in March of 519 BC. You worked for three months clearing the Temple Mount. After working for a month, the task looked impossible. You wanted to quit, but with Haggai's encouragement from the Lord, you and your fellow workers stayed on the job. Finally against all odds, the mission was accomplished. The debris was all cleared.

Today is a big day. The last of the foundation stones are being moved into place. Today the temple's foundation will be completed. Suddenly, the workers grow quiet. Everyone stops. They turn toward a man standing on the foundation. You recognize him. It is Haggai. At first, you are a little uncomfortable. You hope he has good news this time.

Haggai begins in his rich, resonant voice. The workers crowd closer. He has a message from God; no one wants to miss a word.

Haggai begins with a brief summary of his recent two messages that have stirred Jerusalem's entire population. He rehearses your misplaced priorities over the past fifteen and a half-plus years. He also declares God's just chastening.

"He already told us this", you think. "Doesn't he realize that's why we repented? That's why we are here working like slaves."

Even so, you know he's right. He is speaking God's Word. Again, you think of your expensively paneled house with your double lot and gated compound, just two streets over from the base of the Temple Mount. If you stood on a foundation stone that is not yet in place, you could see the brightly colored blue-and-white-striped covering over the sitting area on your rooftop.

You also think of your parched grain fields and vineyard. You remember your sickly crops over the past few years. Your shop has been steadily losing money as well. Suddenly, you feel exhausted and defeated. Your back and legs, arms and hands ache. A friend passes you a skin of water. You take a long drink, but your thirst isn't quenched.

Haggai moves past his introduction and into the heart of his message. Today he questions the priests. He asks them to clarify a purification and corruption law. You feel a momentary relief. At least the target is off your forehead for a moment. Until you realize Haggai's point, God has been just. You have corrupted the economy and caused the drought.

The message turns in a new direction. You can hardly believe it. Your heart jumps into your throat. Haggai has a fresh revelation from God, and it is good news! "'From this day forward,' God says, 'I will bless you!'" (2:19).

If you were that worker, leaning against a huge foundation stone, what would you expect? I would expect my circumstances to change quickly. I would expect the work to get easier, the resources to be abundant, and soft, steady rains to end the drought and multiply my crops. I might not expect complete health, wealth, and ease, but I would expect an immediate change for the better.

Remember, we teach our students that the main points of the text support the text's main theme. Haggai's first main point: *God's blessings do not erase our past.* This fact is a blessing in disguise.

Haggai's second main point may also surprise you: *God's blessings are not always immediate.* Haggai demonstrated this fact with a question and a statement.

Haggai's question: "Is the seed still in the barn?" (2:19).

"Yes." That's obvious.

God promised to bless the crops, but the seed was still unplanted. It cannot produce a harvest in the barn. Haggai drove the point home. "As yet the vine, the fig tree, the pomegranate, and the olive tree have not yielded fruit. *But* from this day, I will bless *you.*"

God's blessing was a reality that day though the visible evidence was delayed. The Jerusalem residents had to take God at His Word and *walk by faith, not by sight.* This happens in our lives as well.

Real Despite Delay

Delayed blessings are real today. We too are called to *walk by faith, and not by sight*. But don't think this is a hardship. God is the one true Promise Keeper. When He announces His blessing, we can count on it. When we live out God's priorities for our lives, we can be assured that God's blessings will flow even if we do not yet see them.

During Jesus's earthly ministry, His followers learned about God's delayed blessings. Mary, Martha, and Lazarus were among Jesus's closest friends and followers. They lived in Bethany near Jerusalem. Lazarus became seriously ill. His sisters sent word to Jesus. "Lord, behold, he whom You love is sick" (John 11:1–3).

Upon receiving the message, Jesus told His disciples, "This sickness is not unto death, but for the glory of God, that the Son of God may be glorified through it. Now Jesus loved Martha and her sister and Lazarus" (vv. 4–5).

Great. We expect Jesus to either head for Bethany immediately or, by remote control, heal Lazarus immediately. The latter seems preferable—the quicker the better. Isn't that obvious? How else could He receive the glory? How else could He demonstrate His love for the family? But Jesus did neither. "He stayed two more days where He was" (v. 6).

On the third day, Jesus said, "Let's go to Bethany."

The disciples said, "Bad idea. Too dangerous. They wanted to stone you the last time we were there."

"Lazarus is asleep. I need to go wake him."

"Sleep is good medicine. If he's asleep, he's getting better. We should stay here."

"No. You misunderstand. Lazarus is dead." Can you see the confusion on the disciples' faces?

When they arrived in Bethany, Lazarus had been dead four days. The funeral was over. The mourning was well underway.

Martha heard Jesus had arrived. She ran to meet Him. "Lord," she said, "if You had been here, my brother would not have died."

Jesus encouraged Martha, "Trust Me. I have power over death as well as disease." She went back to their house and secretly told Mary, "The teacher has come and is calling for you" (v. 28).

The mourners saw Mary rush out. They thought she was headed to the tomb to moan and cry for a while. Good plan. They wanted to help, so they followed her. Instead, she went to Jesus.

Mary and Martha had discussed the situation in detail. They couldn't understand Jesus's indifference to their dilemma. She echoed Martha's statement. "Lord, if You had been here, my brother would not have died" (v. 32).

None of it made sense to them. "Jesus could have done something but didn't. Why wasn't He on the job when we needed Him?"

Mary began to cry. The mourners joined in, and so did Jesus. He "groaned in the spirit and was troubled. Jesus wept." Jesus really does care; He is concerned about our pain. He asked them to show Him Lazarus's tomb (vv. 33–35).

No doubt the disciples were confused as well.

Four days earlier, Jesus announced that Lazarus's sickness was *not unto death, but for the glory of God that the Son of God may be glorified through it.* Now it appeared the opposite had happened. How could this be? Jesus had never been wrong before. Why had He not acted while there was still time? Now it was too late.

No one understood what was going on. No one, that is, but Jesus.

Why?

Can you identify with Mary and Martha? Are you in a similar situation? Are you asking, "Why am I in this mess? Why doesn't He do something? Why didn't He come when I called? Why didn't He answer when I asked? I know He *can*, but I'm no longer sure He *will*. Deep inside, I'm no longer confident that He cares." Or perhaps you identify more with the disciples. You've prayed for a friend. You know your friend and his/her family are praying. The situation is desperate. Your friend is also Jesus's faithful servant and friend. If anyone deserves to be blessed, surely this friend does. But God isn't coming through. Why?

If you are asking some or all of those *why* questions, maybe you are in for a great surprise. Would you consider the possibility that Jesus knows what He's going to do? He may have a plan that you haven't considered. He may be about to do something much better than what you asked. When His surprising answer comes, you'll praise Him for not answering your request. That's what happened to Mary and Martha. The disciples saw it and their faith in Jesus grew.

Jesus's Surprise Answer

Jesus, Mary, Martha, the disciples, and the mourners arrived at the tomb. "Take away the stone," Jesus said.

Martha protested. Lazarus had been dead four days. Without embalming, his body was decaying. The stench would be horrific, but Jesus insisted. With reluctant hands, covered noses, and squint-eyed *stink faces*, some men removed the stone.

Jesus looked up to heaven, thanked the Father for hearing His prayers, and *cried with a loud voice*, "Lazarus, come forth!"

To everyone's wide-eyed, open-mouthed astonishment, the stench vanished, and Lazarus hopped to and through the tomb opening. "He who had died came out bound hand and foot with grave clothes, and his face was wrapped with a cloth. Jesus said to them, 'Loose him, and let him go'" (vv. 41–44).

Suddenly, all their confusion was clarified. All their *why* questions were answered. The sisters were giddy-glad Jesus arrived too late to heal their brother. They were glad for the delay. They were glad Jesus let Lazarus die.

Raising *dead Lazarus* revealed Jesus's power and glory far more than healing *sick Lazarus*. The blessing was delayed so it could be multiplied. When God's blessings are delayed, His children tend to think they have been cancelled. Like Martha and Mary, we know He *can*, but we doubt He *will*.

Desperate Questions

Delayed blessings often prompt desperate inquiries. Self-doubts creep in. "Did I do something to cause the delay? What could it be?" If no answer is found, "Doesn't God understand how bad it is? Does He not realize how much better it would be if He acted? Have I been wrong about God's unfailing love? Maybe He doesn't care after all." Intellectually, we know better. Emotionally, painful delays cloud our minds.

May I suggest three things we can do when God's promised blessings are delayed?

1. *Be honest with God.* Lay your thoughts, feelings, and complaints before Him in prayer. Multiple examples are in the Psalms. He knows

your emotions and anxieties. Your prayer will not shock Him.

2. *Spend time in God's Word*. Read the Psalms. Read faith-building passages like Hebrews 11, along with the background narratives. Note the hopeless situations where God stepped in at the last minute. God's Word is powerful. It gives perspective. It helps us think correctly when our feelings run wild.

3. *Prepare for God to act*. Often, we feel our situation is completely out of our control. Frankly, many things in life are beyond our control. However, we should do the things we can do.

George Mueller

Consider George Mueller. If you have never read his biography, you should. Make it a priority.

Mueller lived in England in the late nineteenth century. The Lord led him to start orphanages to care for and share Jesus with destitute and abandoned children. Mueller believed God directed him never to ask any person for financial support. He simply prayed, asking God to meet his, his staff's, and the children's needs. His biography is one story after another of God's amazing provisions. He made an astounding impact on the orphans, his staff, and the Christian world. He influenced two other Christian leaders greatly—Hudson Taylor and D. L. Moody.

While I recommend the book highly, I want to add a warning: don't revel in the victories and pass over Mueller's difficulties. Carefully read his life story, observing a great example of dealing with God's delayed blessings.

On one occasion, Mueller prayed and prayed for God's provision. He was certain the blessing was coming. Time passed. The blessing was delayed and delayed until his resources dwindle to nothing. A mealtime came when there was nothing to feed the children. Bare cupboards. Empty bank account. Empty pockets.

Mueller had the children set the table and take their places. No food. He led them in prayer. He thanked God for the food He was about to provide. As Mueller finished his prayer, they heard a knock on the front door. A milk wagon had broken down in front of the orphanage. The wagon had to be unloaded. The milk would spoil before they could complete the repairs. The driver asked if they could use the milk. A baker, asking if they could use a wagonload of bread, immediately followed the milk delivery. God's provision was delayed but abundant and just in time.

Mueller not only asked God for help, but he also trusted the promises in God's Word and prepared to receive God's blessing. He kept asking, trusting, and preparing for God's provision. Why? Mueller knew God's blessing would arrive. He also knew that *when* it arrived, it would be delightful!

Delightful Blessings

This is exciting. God's blessings are certain.

God's blessings are as sure as His promises. They are as certain as the sunrise. God cannot lie (Titus 1:2); He will not fail. God's promised blessings

- may be disguised;
- may be delayed; but
- they are assured.

Live consistently with your God-given priorities, and you can be certain His blessings are on the way. It was true for Israel, and it's true for us. Three times the Lord promised His people, "From this day forward...I will bless you" (vv. 15, 18, 19). Though they had failed in the past and they couldn't see His blessings at the moment, their blessings were certain. God promised, "I will bless you! I will bless you! I will bless you!"

At Northeastern Baptist College, the certainty of God's blessing keeps us praying, trusting, and obeying. We pursue our God-given priorities, developing students and sending out graduates with a *scholar's mind*, a *shepherd's heart*, and a *soldier's perseverance*. Though our Lord's blessings are sometimes disguised and often delayed, by faith, we anticipate the delightful day when His certain blessings are visible.

Conclusion

As we adjust our lives to live out God's priorities, we expect God's blessings. We can continue living our priorities despite difficulties and challenges. We can't tell our Lord how and when to bless us, but we can expect Him to bless us because He is faithful.

Application

Take a few minutes to consider what it means for God to bless you. Answer the following questions:

1. Prior to reading this chapter, what misconceptions did you have about God's blessings?
2. How can your past failures be a disguised blessing in your life today?
3. How do you typically respond when God's blessings in your life seem to be delayed?
4. What can you learn from Mary, Martha, and George Mueller about dealing with delayed blessings?
5. How can assurance of God's blessing keep you focused on living out His priorities for your life?

Chapter 5

The Blessing of Living Your Priorities

Part 2

The Northeastern Baptist College marching order is "Pursue God's priorities." Despite difficulties and delayed and disguised blessings, pursue God's priorities. We believe *God's children experience God's supernatural favor when we adjust our lives to live His priorities.*

Therefore, we endeavor to develop students and send out graduates with a

- scholar's mind;
- shepherd's heart; and
- soldier's perseverance.

We look to God for His blessings—His supernatural favor. We do what God called us to do, trusting Him to provide for our needs.

Our marching order is not copyrighted, of course. You can pursue God's priorities for your life. Your church can do the same.

In Haggai's day, the God-given priority was rebuilding the crumbled temple. What is your God-given priority?

Haggai's final paragraph (2:20–23), his fourth and final recorded sermon, addresses one individual: Zerubbabel, the governor of Judah. What if, next Sunday morning, your pastor's entire sermon was directed to you by name? Would it be a bit awkward?

Whether or not it was awkward for Zerubbabel, God promised to bless him in unique ways. I believe the message applies to each of us. It states specific blessings God grants to those who consistently live out His priorities.

He Exposes His Plans

Have you ever wished God would show you what He intends to do? If so, you'll be interested to know that is the first blessing Haggai noted—God exposes His plans to those who live according to His priorities.

In my counseling, both as a pastor and as a college president, several people have said, "I wish God would show me His plans. I want to know what He intends to do."

In response, I ask, "Are you doing the part of God's plan that you already know?"

Normally, God does not show us more of His plans until we act on what He has already shown us.

After hearing Haggai's first message [Aug 19, 520 BC (Hag. 1:1)], Zerubbabel adjusted his life; fulfilling God's assignment became his priority. Next [Dec 18, 520 BC (2:10, 20)], the Lord revealed another part of His plan to Zerubbabel. Someday He will "shake heaven and earth" (2:21). He will fulfill His ultimate plan for the entire world. God said, "I will overthrow the throne of kingdoms; I will destroy the strength of the Gentile kingdoms, I will overthrow the chariots and those who ride in them; the horses and their riders shall come down, everyone by the sword of his brother" (v. 22).

As Zerubbabel faithfully pursued God's priorities, leading the Jerusalem residents in the process, the Lord exposed His plans. And what is that plan?

One commentator noted:

> This is reminiscent of the destruction of Gentile world powers represented in the great image in Daniel 2. There the worldwide messianic kingdom will replace the Gentile kingdoms (Dan. 2:34–35, 44–45). The overthrowing of chariots and the fall of

horses and their riders indicate that this change in world government will be military as well as political. In the confusion of this great Battle of Armageddon (Rev. 16:16–18) at the Lord's second coming (Rev. 19:11–21) many a man will turn the sword against his own brother (cf. Zech. 12:2–9; 14:1–5).[1]

God reminded Zerubbabel that in the future, He will fulfill His promises to David. One day, all Israel's enemies will be destroyed. God will bless Israel with a peaceful, prosperous kingdom. The promised blessings encouraged Zerubbabel to trust God for present blessings.

We, too, anticipate a great future. According to the New Testament, God grafted Gentile believers into His plans for Israel's future. Believing Jews and Gentiles will rule and reign on earth with Christ for a thousand years. Earth's entire population will be under Christ's authority.

Notice a few general facts about Christ's future Millennial Kingdom (Rev. 20:1–6).

- Christ will be the absolute sovereign.
- Satan will be bound.

---

[1] F. Duane Lindsey, "Haggai" in *The Bible Knowledge Commentary: Old Testament*, John F. Walvoord and Roy B. Zuck, eds. (Wheaton: Victor Books, 1985), 1544.

- Tribulation martyrs will be resurrected.
- All resurrected saints will live and reign with Christ for one thousand years; the second death will have no power over them.

Satan will be temporarily released after the Millennium and will suffer total permanent defeat (vv. 7–10). We will enjoy Christ's eternal kingdom with all His saints, past and present.

Adam and Moses, David and Paul, you and the person you may lead to Christ next week will be there too. But most of all, Jesus will be there, and we will worship Him in absolute purity and pleasure for the first time ever.

Revelation 21 and 22 describe some of the joy and wonder and glory of our home in heaven. All who turn from their sin and receive Jesus Christ by faith will experience that joy, wonder, and glory.

Jesus momentarily opened a corner of the veil, giving the Apostle John a peek inside. He saw

> A new heaven and a new earth, for the first heaven and the first earth had passed away, also there was no more sea. Then I, John, saw the holy city, New Jerusalem, coming down out of heaven from God, prepared as a bride adorned for her husband. And I heard a voice from heaven say-

ing, "Behold, the tabernacle of God is with men, and He will dwell with them, and they shall be His people. God Himself will be with them and be their God. And God will wipe away every tear from their eyes; there shall be no more death, nor sorrow, nor crying. There shall be no more pain, for the former things are passed away." (21:1–4)

Other details are added in subsequent verses, but that is our future hope and our future home. Today God does not promise that living His priorities will be easy. We will have opposition.

Challenges will come. Trials may abound. However, God's Word is clear. The trials are temporary. They will pass. One day, we will enjoy eternity in God's presence. No more death. No more pain. No more sorrow or crying. Until that day, He promised to be with us. He promised never to leave us. He will never forsake us; His promises guarantee it.

In addition, He promised to bring times of blessing and refreshing even now. As we live out God's priorities for our lives, He assures us

- today, blessings with trials; and
- in eternity, blessings without trials.

Zerubbabel learned about God's promises and plans for his nation's future only after he adjusted his life to live God's priorities. In other words, do what you know you should do now; God will show you what to do next. We can summarize a personal, present day application. *Faithfully live your God-given priorities and God will expose His plan for your next step.*

He Executes His Promises

God also grants a second specific blessing to those who consistently live out His priorities. He executes His promises. He does what He declares He will do. God is faithful to His promises.

God promised David, "Your house and your kingdom shall be established forever before you. Your throne shall be established forever" (2 Sam. 7:16).

God took the kingdom away from Saul's family but promised to never remove the kingdom from David's family.

The promise will ultimately be fulfilled in the Messiah's eternal reign. The Messiah, of course, is "Jesus Christ, the Son of David" (Matt. 1:1).

When the Babylonians conquered Judah, some thought God had changed His mind. Just the opposite was true. Even then, God fulfilled His promises.

Before Israel entered the Promised Land, God warned through Moses,

> [If you worship idols] you will soon utterly perish from the land which you cross over the Jordan to possess; you will not prolong *your* days in it but will be utterly destroyed. And it shall be, *that* just as the Lord rejoiced over you to do you good and multiply you, so the Lord will rejoice over you to destroy you and bring you to nothing; and you shall be plucked from off the land which you go to possess. (Deut. 4:26; 28:63)

The Lord rebuked one of David's descendants, "'As I live,' says the LORD, 'though Coniah [also called Jeconiah and Johoiachin] the son of Jehoiakim, king of Judah, were the signet on My right hand, yet I would pluck you off'" (Jer. 22:24). Coniah, an idol-worshiping king of Judah, lost his throne. He and Judah went into captivity because of their perpetual rebellion against God.

Still, God did not forget His promises. After seventy years, as promised (cf. Jer. 25:5–13), He took His people back.

Zerubbabel, David's descendant and Coniah's grandson, became Judah's governor when they returned to Judah. Because he adjusted his life and led the people in rebuilding the temple, the Lord said, "I will make you like a signet ring" (Hag. 2:23).

A king wore a signet ring. He used it to impress a wax seal on important documents. The seal indicated the document was the king's property. It had his authority even when he was not present.

The Lord vested His authority in David's descendants. Coniah rejected God's priorities, and the Lord removed him as if removing a signet ring. Zerubbabel adjusted his life to live out God's priorities; the Lord made him *like a signet ring*. God reversed the curse. Though the Persians did not allow Zerubbabel to assume the throne, they did recognize him as governor over the land of Israel. God fulfilled His promise and restored authority to David's family.

Having considered the historical background, notice the personal application for us. When Zerubbabel acted on his God-given priority, God granted specific blessings. Not only did the Lord expose His future plans to Zerubbabel, but He also executed His promises in the present.

His Promises and You

Have you noticed God fulfilling His promises in your life? When was the last time? If it has been a while, have you wondered why? I believe there are at least three reasons.

Distraction. Sometimes God's promises are fulfilled in our lives, but we fail to notice. We are not spiritually in tune with Him. The cares of life distract us. God promised to meet all our needs "according to His riches in glory by Christ Jesus" (Phil. 4:19). Yet too often, we focus on what we don't have and what we wish we had rather than on what God has provided.

Deception. We deceive ourselves into thinking we are *self-made*. We think our intelligence, planning, common sense, or hard work provided what we have. God provides through these, but they are His gifts. He gives abilities and opportunities. According to the Bible, every good gift is from God (James 1:17).

Disobedience. We do not see God's promises fulfilled in our lives because He withholds His blessings. He is chastening us (Heb. 12:5–11) because we have rejected His priorities.

We tend to get things backward. We promise to live God's priorities as soon as He pours out His blessings. If He will give us more money, we will give more to His work. (Surely, He doesn't expect me to sacrifice!) If He sends more people to our church, we will take the gospel to our community. If He will bring more people to our Bible class, we will be better prepared and teach His Word more faithfully. Yet the Bible pattern is just the opposite.

Consider a couple of examples.

- *Elisha's Call (1 Kings 19:19–21)*. The prophet Elijah's ministry was nearing an end. The Lord told him to find Elisha and anoint him to be his understudy and eventual successor. He found Elisha plowing a field behind two oxen. Elijah demonstrated God's call on Elisha. He walked past Elisha and tossed his mantle [a cloak—an outer garment, similar to a shawl] over him. Elisha understood the symbolism and asked for a little time to say goodbye to his family.

  Elisha's next move surprised everyone. He destroyed the tools of his trade. He used the yoke and plow to build a fire. He slaughtered his two oxen, cooked the meat, and gave it to the people in his community. It was a clear sign. He left his old life and livelihood behind. He trusted God to provide for him in the future. He abandoned his old priorities and embraced God's new priorities for his life.

  Through the years, God was faithful to Elisha. God constantly executed His promises on Elisha's behalf (2 Kings 2–13). A similar incident is recorded in the New Testament.

- *Four Disciples Called (Mark 1:16–20)*. Jesus began His earthly ministry by gathering twelve disciples. Two sets of brothers were among the first disciples.

As Jesus walked along the shore, He saw Peter and Andrew casting a net into the Sea of Galilee. They were working professional fishermen.

"Follow Me," He said. They immediately left their nets and followed Him.

He then saw John and James repairing their nets. They too were fishermen. He called them to follow Him as well. "They left their father Zebedee in the boat with the hired servants and went after Him."

These four men exchanged their priorities for God's priorities. They spent the rest of their lives following Jesus and seeing God execute His promises in their lives, their converts' lives, and in the early churches.

Do you want to see God's promises executed in your life? Then adjust your priorities to match His priorities. For you, that may not mean burning your tools or leaving your present employment. Most are not called into vocational ministry, but all are called to be fully devoted followers of Jesus Christ. All can faithfully live out God's priorities in our daily lives. Let's summarize a personal present day application.

Faithfully live your God-given priorities and God will expose His plan for your next step. God will execute His promises in your life.

He Establishes Your Position

Have you thought, "If I had a better position, I could make a difference for God"?

The thought has crossed my mind. It was a generic wish. Maybe your focus is narrower. You long for a specific position. "If I had *that* position," you think, "I'd do a much better job than he's doing. Not having *that* job is the only thing holding me back." Perhaps you coveted an open position. It seemed tailor-made for you, but someone else was chosen.

It's easy for self-pity to fester in your heart. "Why can't I get a break? If someone would just give me the chance, I would accomplish amazing things."

The third principle in Haggai's sermon to Zerubbabel addresses such complaints. When you live out God's priorities, He will establish your position. The Lord assured Zerubbabel, "I have chosen you" (2:23).

God had a plan and position for Zerubbabel, governor of Judah.

The Lord has a plan and position for you as well. He doesn't make everyone like a signet ring with authority to lead a nation, but He does have a position for you.

Zerubbabel did not need to seek a position. He needed to live out God's priorities. He needed to trust God to establish his position.

The same is true for you and me. We need not seek a position in life. We need to consistently follow His priorities and leave our positioning to God.

DR. MARK H. BALLARD

Several years ago, I served as a trustee of LifeWay Christian Resources. Jimmy Draper was LifeWay's president at the time. It was a unique opportunity to interact with Dr. Draper. Many called him *the pastor of the Southern Baptist Convention.*

I observed that numerous people called on him for prayer, encouragement, and advice. Young ministers sought his counsel. Seasoned pastors called for his advice.

Dr. Draper often said, "If a man seeks a position, likely, he isn't qualified to fill it."

Let the Lord position you in His time and in His way.

Another friend echoes this sentiment when he reminds young preachers, "The Lord knows your telephone number." When you are living God's priorities today, you don't need to position yourself for tomorrow. He will position you where He wants you, when He wants you there.

Other Bible Examples

Think of Joseph. He went from a pit in the wilderness to the head of Potiphar's house. Later in a single day, he was exalted from prison to the second most powerful position in the world. David was promoted from shepherding a flock of sheep to ruling as the sovereign of a nation. Nehemiah was promoted from a king's cupbearer to governor of a region. Peter was promoted from a fisherman to a fisher of men. He went from casting nets to being the Apostle leading God's work among the Jews. Paul went from persecuting Christians to being the lead Apostle, carrying the Gospel to the Gentiles.

Billy Graham's Example

God is still in the business of positioning those who follow His priorities.

On March 11, 2018, the Fox television network aired the movie, *Billy Graham: An Extraordinary Journey.* The movie recounted how God took an ordinary sixteen-year-old boy, saved him, called him into service, brought him to a crisis moment of decision, and then constantly positioned Billy where he could be used for God's glory.

Billy's crisis of belief moment came when he was a young preacher. God was using him to lead others to faith in Jesus. But Billy faced a decision about priorities. Some of Billy's friends attacked the Bible's truthfulness. As Billy interacted with those friends, doubts began to trouble him. He knew he could not continue to preach if he did not believe the Bible to be the inspired, infallible, inerrant Word of God. In desperation, he got alone with God in the mountains near his North Carolina home.

Graham read the Bible, prayed, and struggled with God. Finally he laid his open Bible on a rock. He stood back and looked at it. He said, "God, by faith, I accept the Bible as Your inspired Word. I take it by faith." From that moment on, Billy sought to believe the Bible, preach the Bible, and prioritize his life according to the Bible.

As Billy Graham prioritized his life to trust and obey God, the Lord positioned him in extraordinary ways. He preached to more people than any other person in history. He did not aspire to do so, but the Lord placed him before presidents, kings, queens, and dictators. He proclaimed God's Word to the richest of the rich and the poorest of the poor.

As Billy lived out God's priorities for his life, God positioned him to make the greatest impact for the Lord's purposes.

What was true for Joseph, David, and Nehemiah, was true for Peter, Paul, and Billy, and it will be true for you. Humbly live your God-given priorities. God will position you where He wants you when He wants you there. He will position you for His honor and glory, and you will be glad.

As we conclude Haggai's fourth and final sermon, consider three personal applications to your life.

Faithfully live your God-given priorities, and

- *God will expose His plan for your next step;*
- *God will execute His promises in your life; and*
- *God will establish your position in His work.*

God is always faithful. He will never fail. Trust and obey Him, and He will bless you.

Application

Stop! Take a few moments to consider how God's blessings help to keep you focused on living out His priorities for your life.

1. How does God's blessing and your obedience relate to one another in your daily life?

2. What would it look like for you to take the next step in fulfilling God's priorities for your life? How does that step relate to God exposing His plan for the next step?

3. What specific promises do you need God to execute on your behalf as you continue to follow His priorities for your life? Spend a few minutes asking Him to execute these promises in your life.

4. How do you deal with life when you are seeking a position that goes to someone else?

5. What would it look like for you to trust God to establish your position, instead of taking matters into your own hands?

Chapter 6

Back to High School for the Future

It was the first Monday morning of my freshman year in high school. Mr. Brophy walked to my desk. An orange burlap covered corkboard was in his hand. "Mark, what two paces are you going to finish by Thursday?"

Parkhill Christian Academy used the ACE system. Each subject was broken down into twelve workbooks or *paces*. Twelve paces equaled a year of material for each subject. Each student had an assigned cubicle. We worked on paces at our own speed. If a student ran into a problem and could not figure out how to proceed, he or she raised a flag on top of the cubicle. Within a minute or two, a teacher came to help.

The school year was divided into four quarters. A student was expected to complete four paces in each subject each quarter. Every Monday, each student used a goal chart to plan how many pages he or she would complete in each pace that week. One of the teachers checked to be sure goals were set on Monday. Progress toward the goals was checked each afternoon. If the goals were not reached, the student had to take the pace home and complete the goals before the next morning. When a pace was completed, the teacher would take the pace. The following day the student would go to a testing table to take a *subject mastery* exam over the material in the pace. A student received the next pace in that subject, only after scoring 80 or above on the exam. If the student's score was below 80, the student had to repeat the pace.

In addition to the required subjects, the school had fun and interesting extracurricular activities. To participate, one had to complete the required paces. The educational system taught students to prioritize their time and efforts. It also taught students to set goals, evaluate progress, and make adjustments. Numerous rewards served as incentives to stay on track.

"Mark, what two paces are you going to finish by Thursday?"

I responded, "Two paces? Are you kidding me? This is the first week of class."

"I'm not kidding. You must complete two paces this week. I don't care which subjects. That's your call. Now what two paces are you going to finish?"

"Mr. Brophy, I've never completed a single pace in a week. There's no way I could do two paces."

"Yes, you can, Mark. And you will. Not only this week but every week."

"Every week? That's impossible!" I was shocked. "Maybe for some of the smart kids, but I could never do that."

"Mark, this is not negotiable. I'll give you five minutes to look over each subject. Choose two paces. When I come back, we'll post the paces on this board. Then you will figure out what you have to do each of the next four days to make this work. That will be your daily goals. On Friday, you will take your two tests. Then you will decide on next week's paces and develop your plan to complete them."

By the end of the first quarter, God had used Mr. Brophy to teach me about priorities, goals, action plans, evaluation of progress, making adjustments, completing tasks, and enjoying the rewards.

Prior to my encounter with Mr. Brophy, I set my goals, struggled to stay on track, and was always behind. My grades were poor. I was far behind other students my age. Some thought I would never graduate from high school. I suspected they were right.

Mr. Brophy helped me discover a new path. Priorities revolutionized my future. Thirty-six years later, the principles learned in those first few weeks of high school still guide my daily choices. To bring this brief study to a conclusion, consider what your ongoing response to your priorities can be.

Examine Your Priorities

Have you discerned your personal God-given priorities? Obviously, you can't do them if you don't know them.

If you have not yet done so, fold a piece of paper in half. Open it back up. Ask the Lord to show you His top five to ten priorities for your life. At the top of the left-hand column, write "My God-given Priorities." As you seek the Lord, write in that column the top priorities He has given you for this particular season in your life. Some will change as the different stages in your life change.

Some priorities are God's priorities for everyone.

- First, pursue a personal, vital, growing relationship with God the Father through Jesus Christ empowered by the Holy Spirit (2 Pet. 3:9; John 15:1–8; Eph. 5:15–21; 1 Thess. 4:3).
- Second, faithfully fulfill your God-assigned role within your family. The Bible describes different roles and responsibilities for husbands, wives, and children (Eph 5:22–33).
- Third, be a functioning member of a local Bible-obeying body of believers. God intends for every believer to use his or her spiritual gifts to serve and minister to one another in and through a local church (Rom. 12:3–8).
- Fourth, God wants all believers to do their part to evangelize the unsaved and help to incorporate them into the local church (Acts 1:8).

The rest of your list may be unique to you and God's call on your life. The Lord may have called you to be a mechanic, an engineer, a medical doctor, a pastor, a church planter, an international missionary, a construction worker, etc. Whatever God's call for your life, He has equipped you with the personality, skills, talents, and spiritual gifts you need to fulfill His purpose.

Now it's time for the evaluation. Ask the Lord to show you if you are living out His priorities for your life. At the top of the right-hand column, write "My Actual Priorities." Evaluate how you spend your time, your talents, and your treasures. How you use these three resources reveals your real priorities. If the right side is different from the left, make some adjustments. Don't be satisfied with a list. Turn your aspirational priorities into actual priorities; they become the things you actually do.

Live Your Priorities

Second, live your priorities. Twenty-three days after Haggai's first sermon, the people adjusted their lives and began living out God's priorities. You too can adjust your life. Don't wait! Act now! Remember, they

- recognized His presence;
- relied on His promises; and
- responded to his promptings.

The same pattern will help you to adjust your life and begin living God's priorities.

Continue in Your Priorities

Third, continue in your priorities even though it will often be difficult. Many things will come against you. Some will *distract* you. Other things will *delay* you. Still others will threaten to completely *derail* you from continuing to live God's priorities.

Once again, Haggai gave a plan to stay on track. In his second sermon, he encouraged the people to:

- *remember the past*. If God enabled Solomon to build a great temple, He can do it again.
- *rely on God's presence*. When God is with you, He can handle whatever comes against you.
- *rest in God's promises*. He has all power. He owns everything and is able to provide for you. He gave them a picture of a better future.

These three principles encouraged the people of Haggai's day to stay on track and to continue following God's priorities. They encourage us today as well.

Experience God's Blessings

Finally, experience God's blessings. Haggai's third and fourth sermons encourage our life-long pursuit.

Remember, God's blessings *do not erase* our *past*. Often, they are *not immediate*. However, they *are certain*. When you follow God's priorities for your life, you can be certain that He will bless you by

- *exposing His plan*. He will show you the next step.
- *executing His Promises*. He is faithful. You can trust Him.
- *establishing your position*. He has the right position in the right place. He will direct you into it at just the right time.

There remains only one question: will you adjust your life to consistently live out your God-given priorities?

Epilogue

One Day

One day, as he went about his work, a young man reflected on his budding success as a farmer. His career was a genuine joy. His family had farmed their own land for generations. He worked hard and employed several men. The man began working the land as a boy.

Over time, his dad entrusted more responsibility to him. His dad spent more and more time involved in the community while trusting the farm's day-to-day operations to his son.

While the man enjoyed being the boss, he also liked working the fields with the hired men. He didn't sit in an air-conditioned cab on a comfortable seat, riding high above a disk, like our modern farmers tend to do. Instead, he stood on a small platform mounted on the plow, driving a team of oxen back and forth across a hot dusty field. Preparing the field required several teams of oxen with hired servants following their employer's lead. As hot and dirty as the work was, something about being in the field invigorated the young man. Since he worked alongside them, the hired help respected him far more than the average boss.

The man's dad was pleased and impressed. Things were going so well; the senior farmer was considering early retirement. Now he was rarely involved in the business. His son was doing far better than he ever dreamed. He had even broached the subject a couple times.

One day, while the multiple teams were plowing a field, everything changed. All his plans, all his dreams, and all his hopes were interrupted and replaced. In the distance, he saw a man coming. Soon he recognized the preacher.

"What's the preacher doing on our farm?" he wondered.

Spiritually, times were difficult in their nation. Many had turned away from God. False gods were becoming more and more popular. The man and his family, however, were among the faithful. They remained fervent followers of the one true and living God.

Though they had not seen him in weeks, they always enjoyed hearing the preacher. Yet today was unusual. What could he possibly be doing here? He knew it was planting season. Why had he come to visit? Why today?

As the preacher approached, the farmer had the surprise of his life. God had chosen him to replace the preacher. If he accepted the call, it would mean leaving his successful business. It would mean leaving his father's home. It would require him to sacrifice his time, talents, treasures, and comforts. It would mean releasing his hopes and dreams, plans and priorities, and embracing God's priorities for his life. What would he do?

He told his father goodbye. He built an altar. He then took his farming implements, broke them into pieces, and used them to fuel a fire. He offered his team of oxen on the altar. Not only did he sacrifice them to the Lord, he destroyed the tools of his successful trade. The sacrifice declared his new priority to trust and obey God.

Another Day

On another day, early in the morning, two young men sat in a boat with their dad. For generations, their family had carved out a living as fishermen. The business had its ups and downs. Some nights the wind and waves cooperated, other nights it was a challenge just to keep the boat afloat. Some nights their catch was plentiful, other nights it was poor. Some nights they caught nothing.

On this day, they rejoiced. The night's catch had been great. More than once, their nets were on the verge of breaking. At daybreak, they made their way to the wholesaler's dock and sold their catch. Before heading home to sleep, they went back to the shore where they anchored their boat and repaired their nets.

As they sat, mending the nets, their dad spoke, "Boys, I am proud of you! You're becoming fine fishermen and great men. You know how to work hard, trust God, and keep your priorities straight. One day, I'll pass the business on to you boys."

"Look, Dad! Here comes the teacher we told you about. He's the one John the Baptizer pointed out."

Jesus paused, momentarily examining their nets before lifting His gaze to look straight into the eyes and souls of James and John. "Follow Me," He said, "and I will make you fishers of men."

The call demanded a response. It was decision time. What would they do?

To follow Jesus, they would have to change their plans and adjust their priorities. They would have to leave the family business to their dad. What should they do? They did not debate. They did not delay. Immediately, they dropped their nets and followed Jesus. They exchanged their priorities for God's priorities.

Today

As noted in chapter 5, God calls every believer to live out His priorities for our lives. For most, this does not mean leaving one's career behind. Rather most believers will serve the Lord through their careers. However, in every generation, the Lord calls individuals to follow the example of Elisha, James, and John. He calls some to set aside all their plans and even their careers to serve him vocationally.

Today is no different than Isaiah's day. The Lord still calls people to vocational service. Isaiah described his call in the sixth chapter of his book. "Also, I heard the voice of the LORD saying, '*Whom shall I send, and who will go for Us?*'"

Like Elisha, James, and John, Isaiah had to make a choice. How would he respond to God's call?

Notice his response. "Then I said, '*Here am I, send me!*'"

The Lord may be calling you to serve Him through your career. However, don't overlook the fact that He may be calling you to forego your plans, your priorities, and yes, your career. He may be calling you to serve as a vocational church planter, pastor, worship pastor, youth pastor, Christian counselor, or Christian educator. Perhaps He is calling you to be an international missionary or directing you into some other service.

Today may be your day to leave all behind and follow Him! Will you follow?

Northeastern Baptist College

At Northeastern Baptist College, we are training students to have the mind of a scholar, the heart of a shepherd, and the perseverance of a soldier. We focus on helping you fulfill God's priorities for your life. If God has called you to serve Him in the business world, we will help you understand how to fulfill God's calling in your business career. Whether you want to take a single class, pursue an associate degree, or a bachelor's degree in business, we are here to help you. If God is calling you to serve Him as a Christian counselor, Christian musician, or Christian educator, we can help.

NEBC offers individual classes, associate degrees, and bachelor's degrees for your consideration. It would be our joy to help you pursue God's priorities for your life.

Like Elisha and Isaiah, James and John, maybe the Lord is calling you to preach the Gospel as a vocation. If you sense He may be calling you to serve as a church planter, pastor, evangelist, or international missionary, NEBC desires to help you. Our mission is to help you fulfill God's priorities for your life and to do so with excellence.

Don't wait! Take your next step today! You can learn more about how NEBC can help you fulfill God's priorities for your life by visiting us on the web at www.nebcvt.org or by calling today 802-753-7233.

About the Author

Dr. Mark H. Ballard—faithful pastor, diligent church planter, passionate evangelist, innovative educator, creative and prolific author, pacesetting Baptist leader—is the husband of Cindy and father of Benjamin. He graduated from Criswell College with his bachelor's degree and from Southeastern Baptist Theological Seminary with his MDiv and PhD. Dr. Ballard, a native of Colorado, serves as the founding president of Northeastern Baptist College in Bennington, Vermont. Prior to preparing to launch the college, he served as a church planter and pastor in New Hampshire, Virginia,

Florida, North Carolina, and Texas. Mark has filled pulpits, held revival services, and served as a conference speaker in numerous states for more than thirty years.

Timothy K. Christian currently serves as the Pastor at Stamford Baptist Church in Stamford, CT. Previously he served Northeastern Baptist College as the distinguished professor of theology and the director of communications. Prior to coming to Northeastern, Dr. Christian served as a professor and administrator at Mid-America Baptist Theological Seminary. Dr. Christian also served as a pastor, transitional pastor, conference speaker, contributing editor, and coauthor of several works. Tim is married to his lifelong friend and partner, Judy. They have two married children and seven grandchildren.

Ballard and Christian have collaborated on numerous projects, including Bible conferences, outreach training events, regional church-planting strategies, articles, and previous books, including *Normal's Journey* and *Open Doors: The Pathway to God-Sized Assignments*.

CPSIA information can be obtained
at www.ICGtesting.com
Printed in the USA
FSHW020850221119
64298FS

9 781098 005856